DAIRY CO-OPERATIVES AND TRIBAL DEVELOPMENT

DAIRY CO-OPERATIVES AND DEVELOPMENT

A Study of Tribal Dairy Co-operatives in Madhya Pradesh

Dr. R.V. SINGH

PUBLICATIONS

KALPAZ PUBLICATIONS

DELHI-110052

Dairy Co-operatives and Development

Rs.690

ISBN: 81-7835-331-8

Published in 2006 in India by
Kalpaz Publications
C-30, Satyawati Nagar,
Delhi-110052
E-mail: kalpaz@hotmail.com

Lassertype Setting : Rudra Computer Graphics, Delhi
Printed at : Salasar Imaging system, Delhi

Dedicated to My Beloved Wife
Archana Singh
who Inspired Me to Complete this
Uphill Task

Contents

List of Tables

List of Figures and Maps

Maps

Figures

Preface

India has remarkable stride in the dairy development and has first position in milk productuion in the world. In the last four decades a large number of technologies developed in the areas namely animal husbandry, dairy production and fodder production and disseminated nationwide through the various organizations among the dairy farmers.

Dairying, like all agricultural enterprises rests with the individual units of small and marginal farmers those owning two to three heads of cattle and less than two hectares of land. Cattle and buffaloes also provide economic stability to these small farmers in the face of uncertainties associated with agricultural production in complex risk-prone agro-ecosystems of drylands, rainfed areas and tribal areas.

Animal husbandry plays a vital role in supplementing family income and providing additional gainful employment for the weaker sections of our society. In fact, animal husbandry provides more self-employment to the socially and economically disadvantaged sections of society than any other sector.

Madhya Pradesh Dairy Cooperative Federation with the collaboration of National Dairy Development Board (NDDB), a dairy development programme named Integrated Tribal Dairy Development Programme (ITDDP). Dairy co-operatives was established and an institutional framework of co-operative structure not only ensured a ready and regular buyer of milk at guaranteed remunerative prices for tribal farmers but also helped link remote tribal villages with city and urban markets. The impact study of this project is very essential to assess the performance of dairy cooperatives and its effects on socio-economic conditions of tribals. A few questions need to be answered here: How far could the dairy co-operative in tribal village achieve the targets set forth? What benefits do the tribals get? What impact had been found on the beneficiaries of the ITDDP? What problems do they face in successfully running their dairy co-operative? In the present book an attept was made to answer those questions. The findings explored from five districts of Madhya Pradesh in the area of dairy cooperatives and tribal development are well explained in various chapters clearly depict the role of dairy cooperatives in tribal development. Tribal areas of Madhya pradesh exists great potential of developing dairy farming, which can increase the income and employment. The constraints perceived by the tribal dairy farmers and the officials of dairy development programme at the grass-root level need to be plugged by the policy makers to stear and gear further the tribal development in India through dairy cooperatives.

The study will be of immense academic and practical worth on tribal development and dairy cooperatives for the researchers, extension workers, planners, policy makers, administrators and the members of the academic and research organizations.

Dr. R.V. Singh

Acknowledgements

The author takes this opportunity to express his deep sense of gratitude to Dr. M. S. Niranjan for his benevolent guidance and sustained encouragement during the course of this investigation. The year spent in his counsel and company will be always remembered.

The author also wishes to place on record the assiduous help rendered sincere appreciation is extended to Dr. Punjab Singh, Ex-Director, Indian Grassland and Fodder Research Institute, Jhansi (U.P.) for providing study leave for the investigation.

Words cannot express my deep sense of gratitude to Dr. Amar Singh,Addl. Commissioner Extension, Ministry of Agriculture, Govt. of India, New Delhi, Dr. S. Veerasamy, Professor, Division of Agricultural Extension, Indian Agricultural Research Institute, New Delhi, Dr. T. Haque National Fellow, National Research Centre of Agricultural Economics and Policy Research, New Delhi, Dr. B. Barak, Principal, B.V.R.I., Bichpuri, Agra (U.P.) and R. N. Mahapatra, Sr. Research Officer, Tribal Development, Ministry of Tribal

Affairs, Govt. of India, New Delhi for his valuable suggestions.

I would like to express my appreciation and gratitude to the many colleagues and friends who helped me, directly and indirectly, in discussions and many ways .The staff members of Indian Grassland and fodder Research Institute, Jhansi (U.P.) and Tribal Research Institute, Bhopal (M.P.) and National Research Centre for Integrated Pest Management, New Delh are remembered for their ever co-operatives attitude. The financial assistance received in the form of Tribal Research Fellowship in Agriculture, Tribal Development, Ministry of Tribal Affairs, Govt. of India, New Delhi is gratefully acknowledge. The author finally records his gratitude to his parents and family for their patience.

R .V. SINGH

1

Introduction

For over centuries, animal husbandry in India is an essential and well-integrated sub-system of Indian Agriculture. It plays a significant role in rural economy by providing gainful employment, especially to women, landless, poor, tribal people and other weaker sections of our society. Most of the milk production in India is based on efficient utilization of on-farm resources including crop residues and wastes and other farm by-products. This is a unique feature of animal husbandry in India that contributes to the lowest cost of milk production in the world at $ 21 for every 100 litres of milk (Kulkarni, 1999).

In India, dairying, like all agricultural enterprises rests with the individual units of small and marginal farmers those owning two to three heads of cattle and less than two hectares of land. Cattle and buffaloes also provide economic stability to these small farmers in the face of uncertainties associated with agricultural production in complex risk-prone agro-ecosystems of drylands, rainfed areas and tribal areas.

Animal husbandry plays a vital role in supplementing family income and providing additional gainful employment for the weaker sections of our society. In fact, animal husbandry provides more self-employment to the socially and economically disadvantaged sections of society than any other sector (Sahay, 2000).

A cursory look at the livestock statistics worldwide would throw some interesting facts about our country. India occupies the first position in the world in livestock population, with about 51 per cent of world's population of 1420 million. Cattle population comprises 198 million which is about 50 per cent of Asia's livestock population and which is about 15 per cent of world's population (Dairy, 1992).

With regards to milk production, India has been in the second position till 1997, but from 1998, it has become first in milk production in the world. India's milk production is increasing annually by almost 3.5 per cent (Kulkarni, 1999). Now, India has retained its leadership position in milk production with 78 million tonnes of milk in 1999-2000, representing about 4 per cent growth over last year's output (Anonymous, 2000).

Among the different states of India, Madhya Pradesh occupies first position in livestock population especially cattle population. The following Table 1.1 gives an idea of livestock population in Madhya Pradesh in 1992(in thousands).

Madhya Pradesh, being one of the most backward states in India, cannot boast of high

Table 1.1 : Live Stock Population in Madhya Pradesh in 1992 (in thousands)

	Madhya Pradesh	*Male*	*Female*	*Total*	*No. of males/ 100 females*
1.	Cattle-Crossbred	65 (1.37)*	144 (1.36)	208 (4.46)	
2.	Cattle-Indigenous	15102 (15.6)	13378 (14.5)	28480 (29.3)	112
3.	Cattle-Total	15166 (14.9)	13522 (13.1)	28688 (14.0)	
4.	Buffaloes	2556 (14.73)	5414 (8.0)	7970 (9.46)	47

(Figures in parenthesis indicate percentage of all India population)

Table 1.2 : Milk Procurement by Dairy Co-operatives

	State	*Procurement by co-operatives (LKPD)*	*National production (LKPD)*	*Procurement as per cent of production*
1.	West Bengal	51.830	3441	1.51
2.	Madhya Pradesh	90.155	5442	1.66
3.	Haryana	81.395	4527	1.80
4.	Uttar Pradesh	262.435	13552	1.94
5.	Rajasthan	261.340	6150	4.25
6.	Bihar	71.175	3498	2.03
7.	All India	4916.185	74665	6.58

Source : Annual Report NDDB, 1998-99

milk production. But this state has greater production potential that needs to be exploited at the earliest.Milk procurement from dairy co-operative is another dimension of the issue of enhancing milk production in Madhya Pradesh.

The National Dairy Development Board (NDDB) has set an ambitious target of almost quadrupling milk procurement by co-operatives from 1998-99 level of 134-69 lakh kg per day (LKPD) to 488 LKPD by the year 2010. A milk procurement level of 488 LKPD would require the co-operative to mop up 33 per cent of the country's available to marketable surplus, from its current level of 11.7 per cent (which is 134.69 LKPD or 4.92 m.t. per year and which is 6.58 per cent of the country's total milk production).

Quadrupling all Indian procurement levels over the next decades would basically mean replicating the Gujarat formula in other states with much bigger milk production potential as especially, Uttar Pradesh, Madhya Pradesh and Rajasthan, which the co-operatives have not been able to exploit. The following Table 1.2 provides data for a few states in 1998-99.

Milk procurement in Madhya Pradesh is the second lowest in the country while it is highest in Gujarat. A brief look at the history of dairying in India is very pertinent here.

Dairying in India

The Indian dairy industry was not blessed with great many natural advantages. In fact, we suffered from all possible disadvantages. Unfortunately, the policies and programmes during the colonial era ensured that our milk production languished at around 20 million tonnes. Another equally serious problem was that dairy farmers in our village were compelled to sell milk to middle men at derisory prices, simply because milk would not keep beyond three hours in our climate.

In this generally dismal scenario, the farmers of one district, Kheda in Gujarat, under the advice of Sardar Vallabhbhai Patel, formed a dairy co-operative to sell milk directly to the markets instead of through middlemen. This initiative met with fierce opposition from all quarters-from colonial government, local privately owned dairy in Kheda, milkmen who fleeced both farmers and customers.

The new co-operative struggled against all odds for years but it survived and eventually thrived. By 1965, this co-operative-what everyone today knows as AMUL had acquired a name for itself as the best run and most modern dairy co-operative in the country.

In 1965, the then Prime Minister of India, Late Lal Bahadur Shastri, visited Kheda district and decided that the AMUL example should be replicated all over the country.

This led to the setting up of the National Dairy Development Board with the mission of replicating the AMUL experience -what came to be called the Anand Pattern of Dairy Co-operative all over India. Thus the programme Operation flood began with a plan to build four metropolitan daries and to promote dairy co-operatives in 17 promising areas-termed milk sheds in 10 states (Kurien, 1999).

Thus European Economic Community (EEC) played a helpful role in ensuring that the Anand pattern replication succeeded by donating skimmed milk powder and butter oil to India. These commodities were reconstituted into liquid milk and sold in our metropolitan markets.

The money generated from the sale of the gift commodities was used to finance the four metro dairies and to pioneer the establishment of dairy co-operatives to supply them. In the second phase of Operation Flood, EEC commodity support was supplemented by World Bank loans. During this phase national milk grid was establishment, which ensured that major cities all over the country received their milk supplies by rail and road tankers from places as far as 2000 km away. The third phase expanded the effort made to embrace the entire country.

Today, there are 10.1 million farmers who are members of 77000 village dairy co-operative societies, each of which is affiliated to one of 170 district and regional co-operative unions, which in turn, are part of a state co-operative marketing federation. There are 22 of these federations which offer dairy and other products in the market successfully competing among themselves and with dairy firms owned by individuals, investors and multinationals.

Efforts Made in Madhya Pradesh

In the Operation Flood Programme, with the collaboration of National Dairy Development Board (NDDB), Madhya Pradesh Dairy Cooperative Federation, Madhya Pradesh Adivasi Vitta Avam Vikas Nigam and National Scheduled Caste/Scheduled Tribes Finance and Development Corporation (NSFDC), New Delhi, a dairy development programme was in some selected tribal districts of Madhya Pradesh which was named Integrated Tribal Dairy Development Programme (ITDDP). Dairy co-operatives were established and an institutional framework of co-operative structure not only ensured a ready and regular buyer of milk at guaranteed remunerative prices for tribal farmers but also helped link remote tribal villages with city and urban markets. A few questions need to be answered here: How far could the dairy co-operative in tribal village achieve the targets set forth? What benefits do the tribals get? What impact had been found on the beneficiaries of the ITDDP? What problems do they face in successfully running their dairy co-operative? So, a study has been planned with an overall objective of assessing the dairy cooperative in tribal belt of Madhya Pradesh and to know its impact on tribal lives, with the title " A critical study on the impact of Dairy Development Programmes on the Tribals of Madhya Pradesh with special reference to Dairy Co-operatives: with the following specific objectives:

1. To analyse the target achievements of co-operative dairy development programmes in the area
2. To ascertain the opinion of beneficiaries, non-beneficiaries and officials towards co-operative dairy development programmes
3. To study the changes as a result of various schemes of the programme
4. To study the impact on socio-economic conditions of beneficiaries in tribal areas
5. To find out the different problems faced by the beneficiaries and officials regarding the participation and execution of the programmes and suggested suitable measures for improvement.

Scope and Importance

This study aims at getting information on the parameters of impact of dairy co-operative societies on tribal lives. The indicators of achievement studied in this research work will bring to focus the real aspects of impact studies, especially that of dairy co-operatives. So this research investigation has a great scope in understanding the progress of work of any tribal dairy co-operative.

In addition, this study also emphasizes the efficient running of dairy cooperative in tribal areas, the knowledge of which will help in evaluating other diary co-operatives and taking appropriate actions for their better functioning.

Limitation of the Study

Being a student's research project, the present investigation suffers from the usual limitations of time, funds and other constraints.Limitations of time stood as a barrier for deeper probe in understanding the typical tribal setting. However, considerable efforts were made by the researchers to adjust with the situation.

In addition to Ex-post facto design, participant and non-participant observations were also used to understand the tribal setting but complete assimilation could not be achieved because of the fact that the researcher was treated as an outsider. For the information about the information about the socio-cultural setting the researcher had to rely on secondary sources.

The study largely relied on the response of the tribal farmers. They are often reluctant to give precise information on the delicate matters but they were tackled by establishing a through rapport.

The language barrier could not be completely avoided and an attempt was made to get the correct responses by translating the interview schedule in tribal dialects with the help of school teacher, school boys, members of voluntary agencies, officials of the Tribal Dairy Co-operatives Societies and local leaders. Further, correct of responses, quite often depending memory might despite the best efforts of the investigator to leaves some margin for error to creep in.

Some scales, measures and test were used, but due to variation in tribal conditions the administration had to be done with minor modifications.

It is also recognized that this study was conducted in a limited villages, which covered under Integrated Tribal Dairy Development Programme, in five districts of Madhya Pradesh under a specific tribal cultural situation. Obviously, the findings emanating form the study would be applicable in similar tribal pockets, while the general conclusions arrived at, may be of value in other tirbal pockets and developing areas too.

Inspite of the above limitations, the investigation has opened further avenues in these directions. It can also be hoped that, this study would provide a better insight into the problems and farming conditions of the tribals, which may help in formulating better tribal development strategies for the tribal areas.

2

Review of Literatures

Anthropologist and sociologists have studied tribals, in India, at great length but extension researchers have seldom attempted this area. A review of tribal studies has made it amply clear that enough literature is not available to dairy farming and its developmental programme, particularly in tribal milieu. However, keeping in view the objectives of the present study, the review of literature has been presented under the following main heads:

1. Tribal Ethnography in Madhya Pradesh
2. Dairy farming in Tribal Setting
3. The profile of Tribal farmers
   (i) Socio-economic variables
   (ii) Socio-psychological variables
   (iii) Communication variables
   (iv) Impact variables
4. Dairy Farming Practices followed by Tribal farmers
5. Problems faced by beneficiary for dairy co-operatives and officials.

Tribal Ethnography in Madhya Pradesh

The earliest attempts at the tribal studies by British administrators and enlightened scholars in Madhya Pradesh remains confined to the Gonds who obviously, are the largest tribal population of the state. The ethnographic reference about the Gonds and other tribes of Madhya Pradesh also find a place in the census report; Anderson, J.D. (1913) published significant work. The people of India (Cambridge). Hiralal (1926) studied sociological problems of tribals and published the "Marriage Custom' in the in the Central Province". Ghurye (1957) emphasised on an important approach to study the questions of tribes from physical, sociological andanthropological point of view.

Dube (1958) reported that the agents of the rural development projects and programmes of the technical assistance confronted with cultural factors at almost every step in thier work. The acceptance of the agents of change as well as the effectiveness of the media through which they endeavour to communicate their innovations are largely governed by cultural pre dispositions, attitudes and social organization of the community in which they operate. The acceptance of the programme itself is determined to a considerable extent, by a variety of complex cultural factors ranging from simple habits and accepted social practices to the intricate patterns of beliefs, social structure, values and attitudes.

The next significant work of Elwin Verrier (1963) was an outstanding scholar, who explored the tribal area of Mandla and Bastar districts in has own inimitable style. He lived here for 25 years and was able to achieve complete identification with tribals in these parts of the erstwhile Central Province. He published the Maria and their Ghotul (Oxford Univ. Press, London, 1943), Maria Murder and Sucide (Oxford Univ. Press; London 1943), the Aboriginals (oxford Univ. Press, London,s 1943). He emphasized of an integrated approach to study the question of tribals from physical, sociological and anthropological points of view.

Sahay (1969) remarked that the tribal people are at different levels of socio- cultural and economic development and have certain socio-cultural problems, which are in many ways distinct the other rural people. The religious beliefs and practices of the tribal people have a definite influence upon the matter of adoption of new practices. He concluded that the lastes of the people, their habits, institutions, customs, and traditions, to terms, taboos, attitude, norm, values, beliefs, practices and the nature of the society have a very strong influence concerning tribal development and welfare.

Naik, T.B. (1969) published full-length monograph on Bhil. Tribal Research Institute, Bhopal, (M.P.) conducted very vividly research work on tribals' different aspects and also empahsised on an integrated approach to study the question to tribes from developmental point of view. Gulati (1970) examined various factors, which have been responsible for social change among the Bhil. He reported considerable change in the traditional Bhil region, owning to the impact of 'Hinduism' and observed that they proper to be called 'Hindu Bhils'.

Mitra (1977) revealed that the tribal socio-cultural setting in characterised by particular socio-cultural reservations without disintegrating the qualities of culture, the typical of which are the folk art and music, a way of life, which is a perfect expression of ecological balance in nature which has fostered a love of honesty, truthfulness and freedom from inhibition.

Michonl (1978) stated that tribals have survived as a different ethenic group because of the isolation from the mainstream of Indian culture. He further pointed out that tribals have limited aspiration with regard to material and financial progress. For them social relationship, a life in hormony with ones surroundings, matterns more them just earning more.

Sadamate (1978) has indicated that traditional tribal orgnisations are more credible and dominated by traditional religious leadership pattern then other.

Singh (1980) also remarked that by and large, the general concept of tribal development in post-independence India might not fall fully accord with their own perceived ideal system

Vyas and Mann (1980) reported that the tribal heritage provides the soul to many ingredients of Indian culture. And a proper identification of the same is essential in the exploration of Indian social system and cultural heritage.

It can be emphasised that tribals of Madhya Pradesh have been studied ethnographically at great lenght by the sociologist and anthropologist. The Tribal Research Institute, Bhopal (Madhya Pradesh) has published monographs, research studies and research journal on tribals from sociological, economical and antropological point of view.

Dairy Farming in a Tribal Setting

Dairy farming system is studied in relation to four components, viz. socio-cultural setting, the tribal cattle owner, dairy farming practices followed by him, and developmental system with respect to animal husbandry. The review of literature related to these components is given below:

Mathur (1975) stated the quality of animals were poor eventhough it was important occupation of tribal area.

Thaha (1975) stated that major constraints, which find the cattle rearing in the hilly areas, have indetified as shortage of nutritious fodder and poor genetic mortality of cattle.

Franco and Chand (1991) observed the following achievements in dairy farming in tribal setting in Gujarat (i) the itroduction of the buffalo rearing in tribal community (ii) the increase in cattle wealth (iii) the provision of a steady source of income and (iv) the degree of participationby all the tribals in the co-operatives.

It can be safely said that socio-cultural patterns of tribals have peculiarity of their own. Identification and study of such patterns is of great importance for planning and implementing development programme in a tribal setting.

3. The Profile of Tribal Farmers

Review of Literature is presented on the selected traits of selected tribal farmers namely socio-economic, socio-psychological, communication traits and impact variables:

Socio-economic Variables

Age

Age is the important independent variable for determining the impact of dairy development programmes. A brief account of literature regarding age has been presented below:

Kolte (1973) reported that majority of the adopters of the sugarcane growers were of the middle age group. Similar findings were also reproted by Jadon (1973), Sharma (1977).

Vaidya (1977) stated that the more number of the respondents (41 per cent) belonged to age group of 30-45 years, followed by above 45 years i.e. (40 per cent) and 19 per cent below 30 years respectively

Sadamate (1978) observed that young farmers ' participation in farming was very low, i.e., 12.50 per cent only.

Srivastava (1982) reported that heads of Munda families of study area were mostly middle aged. There was not much difference in age groups of the respondents.

On the basis of literature reviewed it was found that most of the studied revealed that majority of the farmers were in middle-aged category.

Education

Education is most important personal characteristics of the dairy farmers for determining the impact of dairy development programmes. It helps evaluating the impact of dairy development programmes; therefore, it is directly related to acceptance of dairy development programmes. A brief account of past work regarding education has been mentioned below:

Jadon (1973) reported that less then one half (48.57 per cent) of the potato growers were educated upto 7th class followed by middle school level education (8th to 11th class), respectively. Similar result was found by Kolte (1973).

Vaidya (1977) revealed that 30 per cent respondents are illiterate, while 20, 20, 11, 10 and 9 per cent respondents are in the categories of primary school, high school, middle scholl, college level and can read and write and write respectively.

Patel (1978) observed that majority of the cotton growing famrers (44 per cent) were educated upto primary level, where as 7.5 per cent of the cotton growers were found illiterate respectively.

Singh and Patel (1981) observed that majority of the tobacco growers (82 per cent) were literate and remaining 18 per cent illiterate. Among literate, majority 58 per cent of the cultivators were having primary education; about 20 per cent had secondary education, while hardly 6 per cent had college level education.

Dongaonkar (1982) revealed that majority of the respondents educated upto primary level (33.75 per cent) secondary (17.50 per cent), college level (6.25 per cent) respectively.

Sangle (1982) observed that formal education of the farmers as a factor was found to be positively associated with adoption.

Gaikwad (1983) seen that 15 per cent of the respondent were educated upto primary level standard, 20.70 per cent respondnets were educated upto middle school standard. The 47.85 per cent of the respondents were educated upto high school level followed by 16.44 per cent upto college level respectively.

George (1984) found that beneficiaries are not adequate aware of the various programmes ment for them. This is mostly due to the pehnomenons of illiteeracy prevailing in the rural area.

Family Type and Family Size

Family characteristic like family type, family size plays an important role in evaluating impact of dairy development programmes.

Studies conducted by Choubey (1972), Somasundaram (1976), Chattopadhyay (1976) and Jetley (1977) observed significant positive relationship between these characterisitics and the use of technology. Kulkarni (1979) had reported that the type of family was not related with the extent of adoption of technology of the tribal farmers.

Gholve (1986) reported that family size was not related with adoption of technology.

Housing

Tamboli (1984) reported that all-most all-tribal farmers (99.33 per cent) were having kaccha house made out of mud only. Similar results were reported by Pandit (1981) he observed that 79.87 per cent tribal farmers had kaccha houses made been out of mud while 23-33 per cent had mixed houses made of bricks and mud.

Material Possession

It was observed in Agresco resport (1973) that 80 per cent of the Adivasi farmers had inadequate ploughs, while only 2 per cent of them had improved ones.

Bhati and Swarup (1974) reported that each tribal farmer owned a soil turning plough but other modern farm equipments were non-existent among these tribals

Occupation

Dubey (1971) reported about 90 per cent of the scheduled tribe live on agriculture, of the 90 per cent agriculture work as among scheduled tribe, 52.00 per cent were cultivators and 48.0 per cnet were agricultural labourers. In a similar study Kalappa (1971) stated that 88.0 per cnet of the tribal farmers were depending on agriculture directly or indirectly.

Raghav Rao (1975) stated that 89.25 per cent of the scheduled tribes were however engaged in agriculture sector either as cultivators or as labourers and about 24 per cent of them as shifting cultivation.

Banerjee (1976) reported that majority of the tribal farmers were having agriculture as their main occupation.

Patel (1978) stated that 89.25 per cent of the tribal farmers were engaged in agriculture sector as cultivator or as labourer and 6 to 7 per cent engaged in secondary sector.

Shatawdekar (1979) reported that farming is the main occupation of adivasis but the conditions are poor.

Pandit (1981) concluded that majority of the tribal farmers 84 per cent had farming occupation followed by those 16 per cent who had farming and other occupation.

Hansda (1981) stated that out of the 45 million tribal people in India 90 per cent i.e. approximately 40 million were agriculturists and 10 per cent i.e. five million were landless agricultural labourers who depended on the sale of forest products for their living.

Kanani (1982) concluded that majority of the tribal farmers 54.67 per cent had farming occupation only. The respondents of farming plus labour work, farming plus handcraft and farming plus cottage industry were 20.67 per cent, 12 per cent and 12.66 per cent, respectively.

Farm Size

Kalappa (1971) concluded that tribal famrers had marginal quantity of land holdings and more than half of the holdings were below 5 acres.

Basu (1975) stated that among the cultivating households there were about 72 per cent tribals who possessed land upto a range of 5 acres. Only and in most of the cases these lands were not fertile for raising good harvest.

Desai (1976) reported that the land holding of tribal farmers wass less than 3 acres.

Almost all the studies in the area of adoption of dairy innovations included farm size as one of the variables. The land size of majority of the respondnets varied from small (Kokate, 1980, Ramachand, 1980, Saini, 1980, Sidhu, 1980, Patil 1981, Sayeedi, 1983, Kokate, 1984) to large holdings (Chander, 1970, Garde, 1980, Singh, 1984). These reports revealed that farmers with different size of land holdings to keep animals.

Sayeedi (1983), Kololgi and Anand (1985), Sheoran (1987), Singh (1987), Kaushik (1988), Singh (1989) and Chaubey (1991) reported positive and significant relationship between land holdings and adoption of dairy innovations, whereas, Dubey (1978) and Hazarika (1983) indicated farm size as one of the negative significant preduction of adoption of dairy practices.

Herd Size

Many researchers also studied the number of animals a dairy farmers possessed.

It was revealed from the studies of many researchers, viz., John (1974), Dey (1977), Malik (1978), Singh and Dubey (1978), Rangarajan (1978), Gite (1980), Kokate (1980), Saini (1980), Sharma (1980), Kaur (1981), Patil (1981), Sarkar (1981), Singh (1981), Subramaniam (1982), Kakade (1983), Mahipal (1983), Sayeedi (1983), Kokate (1984) and Singh (1987) that most of the respondents had small herd size. Garde (1980), Ramachand (1980), Sidhu (1980), Srivastava (1982), Hazarika (1983) and Pawar (1983) stated tht majority of the respondents possessed medium herd size, whereas, Gupta (1976), Chauhan (1979), Chinnaiyan (1979), Walia (1984) and Yadav (1986) found large herd size among majority of the respondents.

Singh (1982), Sayeedi (1983), Hazarika (1983), Kologi and Anand (1985), Singh (1987), Kaushik (1988), Gautam (1989), Mahipal and Kherde (1989), Borgohain and Kokoty (1990) and Chaubey (1991) reported positive relationship between herd size and adoption of dairy innovations whereas, Singh and Dubey (1978),

Garde (1980), Patil (1981) and Rao (1987) reported negative relationship between herd size and adoption of dairy innovations.

Annual Family Income

Income is one of the important personal factors, which shapes the adoption behaviour of dairy development programmes of an individual. High income provides dairy farmers with opportunities and grater influence and wider contact.

Sadamate (1978) concluded that income level of tribal farmers was negatively and signfiicantly related to technological gap.

Pandit (1981) reported that majority of the respondents (54 per cent) were having annual family income from Rs 1001 to 2000 per annum. He found significant relationship between income level of tribal farmers and their adoption level.

Bhati and Swarup (1981) reported that the average income per farm as well as per hectare and per capita of Tharu tribal was very low.

Ray et al. (1981) observed that, results of the study of the implementation of SFDA programme in the Hubli district revealed that programme had a positive effect to some extent on farm income.

Singh and Das (1984) concluded that the IRDP facilitated the marginal and small farmers to raise their income and employment.

Grewal *et al.* (1985) observed that the beneficiaries who had worked as agricultural labourers before IRDP assitance and now did professional tailoring have raised their annual incoem from Rs 850 to 2600.

Awasthi et al. (1986) observed in their study of IRDP that more than 50 per cent of the selected beneficiaries could rise above the poverty line due to bank finance and IRDP.

Jain (1986) found that, dairying contributed the maximum increase in net income, followed by agriculture including irrigation and rural industries.

Hirevenkenagoudar et al.(1988) reported that over 56 per cent beneficiaries were getting 50 to 75 per cent of their family income from dairy enterprise, whereas, 60 to 87 per cent of from beneficaries getting 25 per cent of their income from dairy enterprise.

Social Participation

Social participation is the most important social characteristics of the adopters.

Narayanan (1968) observed that farmers having membership social organisation were better adopters than non-adopters.

Bapat and Brahmbhatt (1976) found that tribal farmers having initiative for participation in different social and developmental activities had a higher income and literacy rate.

Sadamate (1978) observed poor social participation in tribal area. Similar finding was also reported by Srivastava (1982).

Deshpande (1980) reported that there was no association between social participation and adoption.

Sangle (1980) reported that Mahadev Koli tribe in Maharshtra state showed significant relationship with their present farming system and the social participation, whcih has resulted into narrowing the technological gap in their agricultural system as primary occupation and source of income.

Tamboli (1981) concluded that most of the tribal farmers 78 per cent were non-member of any organisation while 19.34 per cent were member of co-operative societies and only 2.66 per cent were member and executive of Gram Panchayat

Chole (1982) observed that majority of the respondents had (67.27 per cent) low social participation followed by medium and high social participation i.e. 28.18 per cent, 4.55 per cent, respectively. Similar type of result was found by Nandre (1986).

Kanani (1982) stated that most of the tribal farmers 66.67 per cent were non-member of any organisation while 20.67 per cent were member of co-operative societies and only 10.66 percent member of gram panchayat.

Credit Orientation

Desai (1976) conducted a study in Dharmpur Taluka of Vasad district in Gujarat and founded on the formal and informal credit source operating in tribal area. He stated that traders, landowners and other well of farmers practice the formal credit business. Shopkeepers in the tribal villages were lenders used to recover the money either in the form of cash or grains and labour. He further observed that formal sources like Bank; cooperatives had not been able to take roots in tribal areas due to the amazing flexibility of informal sources in terms of conditions for credit.

Mitra (1977) reported that pressures on cultivated areas created by the non-tribal extension and modern mode of resource exploitation have throw on traditional tribal economy out of alignment. Thus, the relationship between food production and food consumption in susbistance economy and distrubed in financial stability of tribal community, which led them to the clutches of moneylenders.

Das (1978) explained the phenomenon of indebtedness in tribal areas as "the tribals being simple and gullible by nature are subjected to exploitation by people from various quarters. The petty trades who bring them some essentials like salt, kerosene, cloth, species etc. cheat them right and left etc. exploit them in possible ways.

Michael (1978) has explained the indebtedness phenomenon and added that the hold of moneylenders on tribal communities is well known. The case in which cash is given and only interest is collected without pressure for the actual amount still makes farmer to turn to the local moneylender. He further stated that banks were operating in the tribal areas but the banking habit was taking time to grow. This has the prolonged the existence of village moneylender. The vicious circle of an indebtedness existing for generation in tribal areas, thus, has a good chance of survival for a longer period than expected.

Opinions of Dairy Farmers Toward the Dairy Development Programmes

In social research, opinion of a person or group towards social problems or any psychological object is of a paramount important. The success or failure of many a social reform or technology would mainly depend upon the people opinion towards it. The difference in opinion has been the course of quite a large number of disorganizing factors disturbing the behaviour complex of the people towards a particular social phenomenon under question.

The study of opinion is not only important from purely socialised point of view, but also it has a great practical importance in other common matter of life. The dairy farmers opinion towards dairy development programmes will mostly determine the nature and extent of their involvement and participation in transmitting and availing the same.

Prajapati (1988) observed that majority of the banana growers (56 per cent) had favourable towards improved farm technology, while 44 per cent banana growers expressed their opinion unfavourable respectively.

Chole (1982) found that majority of famers i.e. 72.72 per cent respondents had exhibited favourable opinion while 23.64 per cent showed unfarourable opinion towards improved agricultural technology, only 3.64 per cent respondents held neutral towards improved technology in agriculture, same type of resuts were found by Chitnis (1983), Kotikhane (1986).

Knowledge about Dairy Production Technologies

Knowledge is a necessary requirement for occupational socialization of farmers. It is the baiss for any action, which must precede the act of adoption profitable application of modern dairy technology, supposes adequate knowledge and necessary skill as pre-requistic. Needless to say that use of dairy innovations will depend upon acquired knowledge, which is an important component of adoption bheaviour.

Pawar (1983) found that 55.50 per cent of the ordinary members had high knowledge level wheras 44.50 per cent had low knowledge level. They further reported that 56.50 per cent of the ordinary members were high adopters.

Kakoty (1980), Singh (1982), Srivastava (1982), Subramanian (1982), Kologi and Anand (1985), (1987), Nataraju and Channegowda (1987), Kaushik (1988), Gautam (1989) and Borgohain and Kakoty (1990) reported that knowledge about dairy innovation was positively associated with the adoption of improved dairy practices.

Adoption of Dairy Production Technologies

No systematic attempt was made in the past to study in length the breeding, feeding, management and animal health care aspects of the cattle in tribal communities. However, some sporadic efforts had been made by Dannely (2927), Kirtikar and Basu (1935), Hussain (1950) and Chopra et al. (1965). Verma (1966), however, made an indepth study of dairy husbandary practices of nomadic "Gujjars" In Himachal forest ranges. He reported that Gujjars did not allow to calf to suckle the dam for the first milk called colostrum, as they felt that the calf would develop diarrohea. They also did not wash the udder before milking or allowing calf to suckle. He found that tribals generally did not keep cows for milk and bull rearing was a rare phenomenon.

Srivastava (1982) reported that the following tradiational cattle husbandary practices were being followed by tribal "Mundas" of Bihar: (i) Generally tribals did not practices naval cutting and left it to fall itself after a few days (ii) After calving placenta was buried by majority by majority of the respondents (iii) Tribals did not allow their calves to suckle the dam for the first milk called colostrum, (iv) Castration was done by outdated method (v) In isolated village of the study area, non of the tribals never caleld a veterinarian treatment. They believed the disease were caused by supernatural power (vi) Tribal "Munda" treated their animal with local medicines and method for different diseases.

C. Communication Variables

Extension contact

The contact with changes agent is an important factor for adoption as it provides the famrers with complete knowledge about the innovations. It was reported by many researchers that majority of the respondents had medium level of extension contact.

Chahal (1980), Singh (1984), Rao (1987), Kaushik (1988), Gautam (1989), Mahipal and Kherde (1989), Singh (1989), Borgohain and Kokoty (1990) and Singh (1990) found extension contact to be positively and significantly related with adoption.

Mass Media Exposure

Mass media communications are among the most effective methods for creating awareness about an idea or practice. The exposure to mass communication channel constitutes learning experience and gain in knowledge of farm innovations which may lead to adoption of new practices.

Singh (1982), Subramanian (1982), Hazarika (1983), Rao (1987), Kaushik (1988), Mahipal and Kherde (1989), Singh (1989), Borgohain and Kakoty (1990) and Singh (1990) reported that mass media was positively related with adoption of improved dairy practices, while Garde (1980) Sayeedi (1983) and Singh (1984) reported non-significant relationship between mass media and adoption of improved dairy practices.

Milk Production

Most of the studies were attempted to find out the milk production of the household by ascertaining from the respondents milk yields of the day prior to the data collection. The levle of milk production varied from low to high depending upon the area, type of respondents and time/ session of data collection. Chander (1970), Chauhan (1979), Subramaniam (1982), Singh (1983) and Sharma and Singh (1986) reported a higher level of milk production among a large percentage of respondents. Whereas, medium level of milk production among the majority of the respondnets was observed by Gite (1980), Kokate (1980), Hazarika (1983), Sayeedi (1983), Singh (1986) and Yadav (1986) respectively. Chahal (1980), Garde (1980), Sidhu (1980), Patil (1981), Pawar (1983) and Kokate (1984) found that milk production was low among majority of the respondnets.

Chahal (1980), Saini (1980), Patil (1981), Kololgi and Anand (1985), Borgohain and Kokoty (1990) and Chaubey (1991) stated positive and significant relationship between milk production and adoption of dairy innovations.

Milk Sale

The studies coinducted by Chauhan (1979), Chahal (1980), Hazarika (1983), Singh (1983) and

Sharma and Singh (1986) indicated that more quantity of milk was sold regularly by majority of the respondents, whereas, John (1974) and Kokate (1984) found that milk sale was low in their respective study areas.

Kololgi and Anand (1985), Kaushik (1988), Singh (1989) and Chaubey (1991), reported that milk sale was positively related with adoption of dairy practices.

Changes in Socio-economic Conditions of Tribals

Socio-economic conditions refers to the position, a dairy famrer or his family occupies in comparison to others with respect to possession of land, education, type of house, material possession, occupation, farm power and level of social participation.

One of the most important aspect of the organisation or sturcture of any social unit centres on the members who are differentiated on the basis of social positoins they occupy. Social-economic condition is an indication of ones position of command and it may either inhibit or enhance a person's ability.

Financial position of the dairy famrers was significantly an important factor on determining the extent of availment of benefits of dairy development programmes. It is therefore held that farmers with higher income are likely to respond more favourably to new dairy development programmes. High income ensures greater capacity to sustain loss or enables one to invest more for higher economic benefit and thereby augment chances of higher level of availment of benefits. It was therefore; felt that dairy farmers' annual income would influence availment of benefits of dairy development programmes.

Changes in socio-economic conditions of the dairy farmers occur as a result of availment of benefits of dairy development programmes. Barnabas (1969) reported changes occured in the life of most of the villages. The aspects were food habits, clothing pattern, farming, material possession, and education for girls and yield level of crops.

Patnaik (1972) reported that the tribal people did not forward in the matter of treatment of cattle diseases due to certain superstitions beliefs. Inspite of the drawbacks of the various programmes of community. Development, the fact that there had been a great deal of change in the economic life, social custom and behaviour of the tribes of Ruruban could not be derived. Much of the income was spent on expensive clothing and personal adornments. Fine mill cloth and plyster had replaced traditional coarse handloom cloth. The old pattern of dressing had given way to different urban style. In weekly market, paddy, groceries and vegetables were most important items on which most of the businesses were transacted. Payment of dowry became part of the marriage complex.

Agrawal (1977) reported that as a result of adoption of innovaitons, the housing conditions, education of family etc have changed.

Sangle (1977) reported that due to adoption of new agricultural technology the level of living of farmers in irrigated area had improved. Further, he stated that the per capital income, consumption, expenditure can different items like food, clothing, and education health and socio-religious functions increased.

Ray *et al.* (1982) concluded that the training and visit system has brought a rising trend in employment and tosome extent in farm income of the tribal farmers of Hooghly district of West Bengal.

Kuttykrishnan (1985) found that most of the poor households were clsoed to the pvoerty line and various IRDP schemes were capable or bridging the income gap to some extent.

Based on the above-cited literature, it has been asumed that there would have occured changes in the social, cultural and economic spheres of tirbal life due to the implementation of developmental programmes also.

Problems Faced by the Beneficiaries of Dairy Farming

Giridhar (1967), National Commission on Agriculture (1976) and Singhal (1978) reported that the presence of a large number of scrub bulls was a major constraint in the success of artificial insemination.

Ghosh (1974) reported tht and non-availability of feeds and fodders as serious constraints, which the poor famrers were facing.

Kohli (1978) reported the following problems in dairy co-operatives which hinders its growth (1) Management was in a handful of elected members was has had no knowledge of management skill, and (ii) lack of proper organisation and coordination.

FAO (1981) evaluation misson observed someof the problems in dairy cooperatives, which care as follows:

(i) Frequent transfer of officials.

(ii) Excessive government intervention in financial matters like pricing.

Shah (1981) observed that the positions of power merely reflect the power structure existing in village. The chairman and the secretary of dairy cooperatives are generally from the local dominant caste/community.

Tyagi and Mishra (1982) indicated were (i) the respondents viewed that they accepted dairying for meeting domestic requirements (ii) daiyring required a hug capital investment (iii) the artificial insemination is valued as unnatural act and thus should not be practicised, (iv) the respondents felt dissatisfaction with function of AI Centers particularly because non-availability of veterinarian/Slockman, shortage of good quality semen and distant locations of AI centres (v) the veterinary facilities are not evenly distributed to all villages (vi) non-availability of fodder seeds, irrigation and low fodder yield (vii) the cattle owners were found to have a feeling that scientific know how is difficult to be obtained and difficult to be applied in their situation, further, they felt that the scientific know-how requires more money, (viii) unawareness about the existence of vital agencies working for dairy development and (ix) lack of milk marketing security.

Vithal (1986) reported accute water and fodder problem, lack of transport facilities and lack of adequate trained staff as constraints to the success of dairy co-operatives.

Gopala Krishnaiah and Pocahiah (1989) revealed that majority of the respondnets percieved low price of milk for a litre as a main problem followed by delay in payment. There was no provision of loans for purchasing cattle.

Raju and Pochaiah (1991) reviewed the following constraints in percieved by the farmers (i) lack of knowledge of social participation (ii) farmers were not oriented to scientific techniques and economic motivation.

Suggestions for Improvement

Shah (1996) observed member producers suggestions regarding the smooth functioning of the society viz., provisions of loan faclities for the pruchase of milch animals and construction of cattleshed, provision for the feed and fodders on credit basis at susbstantial rates, extension of veterinary and health care facilities, timely and regular payment and hike in the existing milk rates.

3

Research Design

This chapter deals with the various procedures followed in conducting this research investigation. They are presented under the following sections.

1. The setting
2. Locale of the research study and sampling procedures
3. Variables and their measurement
4. Data collection
5. Statistical Analysis

1. The Setting

Since this study was conducted on the dairy cooperatives of tribal people of Madhya Pradesh, an attempt has been made to understand the research setting comprehensively.

Madhya Pradesh is the largest state of India with an area of 44, 43, 446 sq. km. and a population of 6, 61,81,0000 according to 1991

Madhya Pradesh

Tribal Cultural Zones

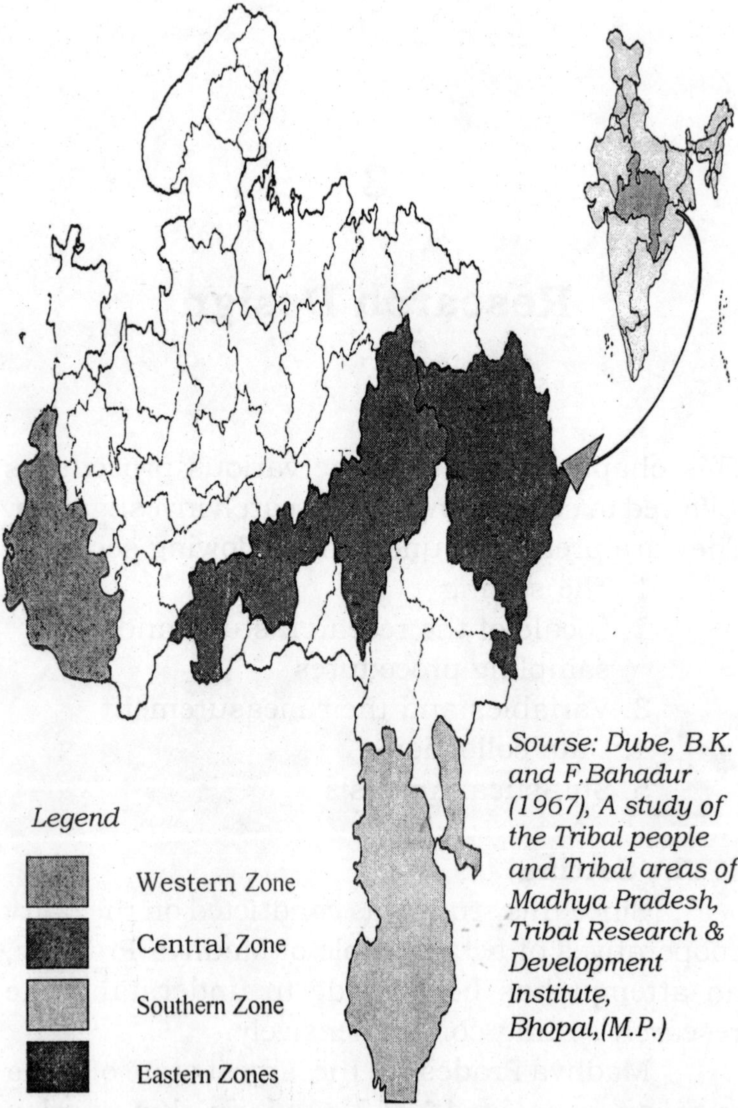

Sourse: Dube, B.K. and F.Bahadur (1967), A study of the Tribal people and Tribal areas of Madhya Pradesh, Tribal Research & Development Institute, Bhopal,(M.P.)

census. This state also has more area under forests, to the tune of about 1.7 million hectares.

The Department of Tribal Development, Madhya Pradesh Dairy cooperative Federation, with the collaboration of National Dairy Development Board (NDDB) had launched a massive dairy development programme-Integrated Tribal Dairy Development Programmes (ITDDP) in 13 tribal districts of Madhya Pradesh. The districts are Bastar, Betul, Bilaspur, Chhindwara, Dhar, Jhabua, Khargone, Mandla, Raigarh, Surguja, Seoni, Shahdol and Sidhi see map of these zones in Map 3.1.

Out of these thirteen tribal districts, this study covers five districts viz., Bastar from Southern tribal zone, Sarguja and Raigarh districts from Eastern tribal zone, Mandla district from central tribal zone and Jhabua from Western tribal zone.

Southern Tribal Zone - Bastar

Location & Topography. The zone is full of rugged hill and plateaus. The Bailadila or the 'Bullock hump' is the highest peak of Bastar district, its highest point being about 4000 feet above sea level.

Climate. Temperature in winter ranges between 12.5°C to 15°C in larger part of the zone and 10°C to 12.5°C in southern Bastar. Summer temperature varies between 37.5°C to 40°C in the larger part and 40°C to 42.5°C in the Northern part; the zone has a annual rainfall ranging between 140 to 160 cms, except in south Bastar Abhujhmarh where it is over 160 cms.

Soil. The zone has sandy red soil. The classification of the soil current among the people of the area is (1) Matari, (2) Kali, (3) Marhan. Kali is rarely found. The position classes recognised by the people are Beda or low lying land, Sum or levelled land and tikrh or high land.

Land use. In Bastar, forest (all type) account for 70.52 per cent of the area of the district. However, since the population in sparse, per capita net area sown is 1.3 acres.

Main crops. The main crop in Bastar is rice of the total cropped area, respectively 13 and 16 per cent under kodon and kutki in Bastar. Oilseed and pulses account for about 6.09 and 9.21 per cent of the total cropped area in Bastar district.

In hilly areas kodon, kutki, Mandia or light mountain paddy are grown in considerable quantities.

Cultivation practices are not yet advanced. Paddy is sown, by and large by broadcasting. Agricultural implements are of primitive type. Shifting cultivation is in vogue in Abujhmar are a of Bastar district.

Livestock. Tribals keep cows, buffaloes, goats, pigs and poultry. The bullocks and male buffaloes (sometimes cows also) are used for agricultural purposes. The higher number of livestock however, does not mean much. Their quantity is poor and the economic return from them is low. Diseases take a heavy toll. A larger percentage of cows are dry and the rest of them yield little milk.

Forest. Forest in this zone and especially in Bastar is very rich. The specialty of the tract is that it has good quality teak as well as sal forest. The teak dominates in the southern parts whereas sal (shorea robusta) covers rest of the area. God quality patches of mixed forest are also dotted over the area. The common tree-associates of teak as well as sal, like Saj (*Terminalia tomentosa*), Seja (*Lagerstoremia parviflora*) and Bija (Pterocarpus marsupium) are also found.

A variety of minor forest produce is available in the area Gum, phoolbahari, mahua flowers and seeds, coccons, harra are some of the more important ones. Tamarind, Chironys and Tendu leaves are also produced in appreciable quantities.

The people. The two main tribes viz., Gonds and Halbas together form about 86 per cent of the tribals' population of the zone. Besides these Kawars, Binjhawars, Sawars, Kamars and Bhattras are some of the other important tribes.

Eastern Tribal Zone-Sarguja and Raigarh

Location and Topography. Physiographically, the zone consists of numerous hills and undulating plateaus. Approximately, half of the area of the zone lying north east to south-west, with an altitude of 1000 to 2000 feet, form an irregular rectangle bound on the south-east and east by plateaus of Manipat, Jamirpat, Hetghat hills and on the south-west and north-west by maikal ranges of the Satpuras and cliffs of Sidhi district.

The larger area of the zone falls in the catchment of the Mahanadi. The main tributaries of Mahanadi are Hasdeo and Mand, which rise respectively in Sonhat and Manipat plateaus of Surguja. The northern portion of the zone, lying in Surguja and extreme eastern part of the zone in Raigarh and Surguja districts fall under the drainage system of the zone. The Kanhar and Rihand are the main tributaries of the Sone.

Climate. In winters, the temperature of northern part of the zone, embracing the whole of Surguja district, except the southern tip, varies between 7.5°C to 10°C. The summers are coolest in central eastern Surguja and northern Jashpur (Raigarh) with 35° to 37°C. The average annual rainfall varies between 120 cm over 160 cms though the larger part falls under the zone where the average annual rainfall is over 140 cm.

Soil. The zone has largely red soil with sandly texture. Local people of Raigarh and Surguja classify the soil into (1) Matasi (yellowish clay soil) (2) Kanhas (black soil) (3) Dorsa (mixture of Kanhar and Matasi (4) Bhata (poor red soil with pebbles) Matasi, which is good for paddy cultivation is found in the eastern half of Surguja district and Gharghonda and Dharmjaigarh tehsil of Raigarh.

Land use. As the tribal areas in Gharghonda, Dharmjaigarh and Jashpur tahsils are hilly and full of forests and have little irrigation facilities, the per capita net area sown and area sown more than once are considerable lower. Similarly, per capita gross value of agricultural output is also lower. In Surguja, area under forests (all types) accounts for 52.06 per cent of the district area.

Main crops. The main crops in Surguja and Raigarh are rice, Kodon-Kutki, oilseeds and pulses. Rice and kodon-kutki are grown in over 49.91 and 10.64 per cent areas in Surguja and 63.08 and 8.60 per cent areas in Raigarh. Oilseeds and pulses account for 9.52 and 14.39 and about 4.74 and 15.33 per cent of the total cropped area in Surguja and Raigarh respectively. In the hilly areas, kodon-kutki are grown in considerable quantities. Cultivation practices are not yet advanced. Paddy is sown by the broad casting method.

Livestock. There is a higher population of livestock in the area. However, the quality of the cattle is poor. The proportion of dry cow is high, and otherwise also, the yield of milk is very low, cattle graze on grass, which is abundant in rains and early winters, or on hay. Paira rice roughage is also used for feeding.

A cattle rearing is uneconomic as mortality is high. The tribal love their cattle but have not realised its economic value. The number and quality is inversely related. There is a great need for improving the breed of the cattle to provide sturdy stock to the tribal cultivators.

Forest. The tract in Raigarh and Surguja is rich in forest; about half of the area is covered with forests. These are in general composed of a mixture of semi-ever-greens and deciduous species. The forests can be classified into two groups i.e. sal and mixed forests. Sal is the dominant spices of the area. The other important trees associated are Bija, Saj, Dhavda, Bhirra, Tendu and Salan.

The zone is equally rich in minor forest produce Mahua and Tendu leaves, Kathha, gum and harra are produced in considerable quantities. Medicinal herbs are also plentiful, particularly in Surguja. Among other minor forest produce of area are honey, hides and horns, Bhilwa fruits, baheda, aonla, chiraita, kosa cocoons etc.

The people. The three main tribes namely, Gond, Oraon and Kanwar together form 76.4 per cent of the total tribal population. Besides these Nagesias, Bharias and other sub-groups, Korwas, Khairwars, Majhwars, Bhainas and Dhanwars, Kharias, Bhainas and Baigas are the other numerically important tribes of the zone.

Central Tribal zone - Mandla

Location and Topography. The Satpura ranges in the east and northeast as well as in the southeast corner cover a larger part of the zone. The zone is bound by the Mavkal hills and the Mahadeo hills lie in the western portion of the zone. About two - thirds of the zone is covered by these hills and has an altitude between 2000 to 3000 feet above sea level with interspersed areas over 3000 feet. The zone falls in the catchment area of the Narmada.

Climate. In winters, the temperature varies between 10°C to 12.5°C except in Mandla, summer temperature varies between 37.5° to 40°C in the larger part East-West of the zone but in the northern and southern parts it is hotter with 40°C to 42.5°C and rainfall in this zone between 100 to 120 cms.

Soil. Various soil and sub-soil types inter-blended with other zonal soils are found in this zone. Mandla has red soils mostly sandy in the eastern and southern parts, but clay in the central parts. Northern Mandla has, however, black soil with clay texture.

Land use. Net area sown is 46.92 per cent of the district area 46.23 per cent area in under forest (all types) account for 33.39 per cent of the total area. Percentage of double -cropped area to net area sown is 23.6 percentage of irrigated area to net area sown is 0.2 per capita net areas sown is 1.3 acres.

Main crops. The zone has both Rabi and Kharif crops. Rice is main crop, However, Kodon-Kutki, gram and oilseeds are the principal crops in this area.

Livestock. In most of the tribal area, livestock population exceeds the human population. However, the quantity of the cattle is poor. The proportion of dry cows is high and otherwise also, the yield of milk is very low. Cattle usually graze or are fed by grass or hay. This rice tract, the roughage is also used for feeding. However, in the summers feeding of cattle becomes a problem. Mortality is high and very often loss of bullocks is the greatest drain on tribal's income and one of the important causes of indebtedness.

Forest and Forest Produce

Teak and mixed forests are found in this zone. The commonest species in these forests are Saj (*Terminalia tomentosa*), Lendia, Dhaora (*Anogeissus latefoilia*), Bija (*Pterocarpus marsupium*), Tendu (*Disopyros melanoxylon*), Mahua (*Bassia latifolia*), Palas (*Butea frondosa*), Harra (*Terminatta ehebula*), Aonla (*Phyllanthus emblica*) etc. Bomboo (*Dendrocalamus strictus*) is found in this zone. Among the minor forest produce available in the forest of this zone, lac, harra, gum, khair (catechu) and mahul leaves are important.

The people. The Gonds (including their sub-tribes) are numerically largest. Out of the local tribal population 71 per cent are Gonds. The other important tribes are Baiga, Kol, Korku, Pardhan and Bharia and Bhumia besides other sub tribes.

Western Tribal Zone - Jhabua

Location and Topography: The tribal areas included in this zone form a contiguous tract, which consists mainly of hilly and sterile land though the general topography of the region presents some varied features. The hilly area, lies between 1000 to 2000 feet. The whole of Jhabua district lies in the mountainous regions of Malwa, which is known as Rath.

Climate: The climate in the region is subjected to greater extremes of heat than the neighboring Malwa region. The cold season is of short duration. The temperature in winters varies between 10°C to 12. °C in a larger part of southern Jhabua. Jhabua get 80 to 90 cms rainfall annually.

Soil: In Jhabua black soil with clay texture is found. The western fringes of Jhabua have red soil with loamy texture.

Main crops: Throughout the zone, the pattern of crop sowing is the same. The Rabi and Kharif, locally known as kurai and chowmasa, are the two agricultural seasons. The main crops. Raised in Rabi season are wheat, gram and sugarcane. In kharif season, the main crops are jowar, maize, soybean, paddy, pulses, oilseeds and cotton.

Livestock: The quality of cattle in this zone is better than that of the cattle in other tribal areas of the state. This bovin population exceeds the human population in this zone also. The quality of cattle is poor in Jhabua and their high number is a great strain on the scarce fodder resource. Feeding of cattle is a problem, especially in summers. The milch cattle become weak and the yield of milk is greatly reduced.

Forests: The percentage of forest area has fallen to alarmingly low levels. The forest in this zone is mainly of a mixed type. Bamboo and grass are important forest produce available in the tract; good quality fodder grass is available which is sold in the adjoining districts of the state. The important minor forest produce is kullu gum, honey, wax, pam rosha oil and tendu leaves.

The People: This zone is the land of the Bhils, who form numerically the second most important tribe of the state, the first beeing the Gonds. The Bhils including Bhilalas, Barelas and Pateelias and other sub-tribes. The above description of the setting has given a through understanding of the study area.

2. Locale of Research and Sampling Procedures

This study "Impact of Dairy Development Programme on the Tribals of Madhya Pradesh with special reference to Dairy cooperatives" was conducted in five tribal districts viz., Bastar, Mandla, Raigarh, Surguja and Jhabua.

These five districts were purposively selected from four zones of the state-central, southern, western and eastern zones, and the criterion followed was maximum density of tribal population.

From each district, five villages were randomly selected. The list of the villages can be seen in the Map 3.2. The list of the villages was taken from the milk union at district level. From each village, the Tribal Dairy Cooperative Society (TDCS), it records, members and their views and responses formed the focus of study.

Selection of Respondents

From each village Tribal Dairy cooperative Society, eight respondents were selected out of

Madhya Pradesh

Study Area within the Tribal Cultural Zones

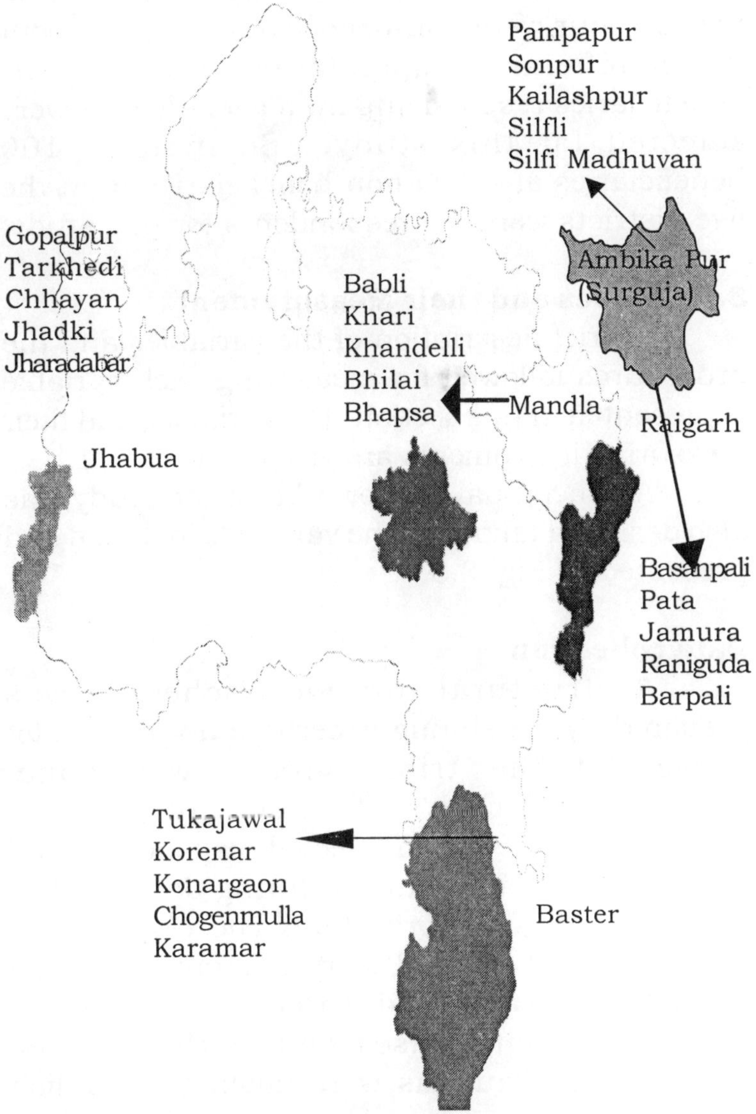

which two each represented the four categories of villagers-landless, marginal, small and large farmers. Out of the eight respondents from each village, four were members and beneficiaries of village Tribal Dairy Cooperative Society (TDCS) and the rest four were non-beneficiaries. Thus, about 20 beneficiary respondents and 20 non-beneficiaries respondents from each district were selected for this study. So in total 100 beneficiaries and 100 non-beneficiaries from the five districts were the respondents for this study.

3. Variables and their Measurements

A brief description of the variables and the procedures followed for measuring each variable is presented in this section. The variables and their measuring instruments are given in Table 3.1.

A conceptual frameworkd of the study was also designed taking all the variables included and presented in Fig. 3.3.

Data collection

A structural interview schedule was prepared by consulting experts and after a pilot survey of the tribal village was done.

The research data were collected by personal interview from selected respondents and reliable secondary sources during Jan 1998 to August 1998 and April 1999. The respondents were contacted at Tribal Dairy Cooperatives Union (TDCU) and Tribal Dairy Cooperative Society (TDCS) at their houses and at their farms. Necessary precautions were taken to establish

Table 3.1: List of Variables and their Measurement

S. No.	*Variables*	*Measurements*
A.	**Socio-personal variables**	
1.1	Age	Chronological age in years
1.2	Education	Modified scale of Trivedi (1963)
1.3	Family type	- do-
1.4	Family size	Scheduled Developed
1.5	Housing	Modified scale of Trivdei (1963)
1.6	Material Possession	-do-
1.7	Occupation	Scheduled Developed
1.8	Farm Size	-do-
1.9	Herd Size	-do-
1.10	Annual Family Income	-do-
1.11	Social Participation	-do-
1.12	Credit Orientation	Scale developed by Sripal (1983)

(Contd.)

(Contd.Table 3.1)

S. No.	*Variables*	*Measurements*
1.24	Nutritional standard of herd	-do-
1.25	Economic performance	Scale developed for the study
1.26	Problem faced by beneficiaries	Scheduled developed for the study
1.27	Problem faced by officials	-do-
1.28	Suggestion for improvements	-do-

rapport and to obtain reliable and relevant information. The cooperation of the president of TDCS, supervisors of TDCS, TDCU employees, TDCS employees and formal and informal leaders of the areas availed whenever felt necessary.

Statistical Analysis

The data were analysed by applying suitable statistical techniques in a systematic manner to get the results.

The data collected from different categories of respondents through schedule were coded, classified, tabulated and analyzed in order to make the findings meaniffful. The data analysis was done at the computer centre of Indian Agricultural Research Institute (IARI) New Delhi. For interpretation and drawing inference the statistical method used were:

Mean

The arithmetic mean is the result of sum of items in the series divided by the number of items and the formula is:

$$X = \frac{\Sigma x}{n}$$

where,

X = the arithmetic mean
Σ = The summation

x = each individual item in the series

n = Total number of items in series

Standard Deviation

The standard deviation is found by taking the difference of each item in the arithmetic mean (x), squaring this difference (Σx^2), summing all squares differences (Σx^2) and dividing by the number of items (N) and then extracting the square root. The formula is:

$$\sigma = \frac{\sqrt{\Sigma x^2}}{N}$$

where,

σ = thestandard deviation

Σ = the summatio

x^2 = the sum of square deviation from mean

N = the number of items

Coefficient of Correlation

This test as used to find out zero-order correlation between dependent and independent variables to know the degree of linear relationship. The formula used for calculating coefficient of correlation was as follows:

$$r = \frac{N\ \Sigma xy - (\Sigma x)\ (\Sigma y)}{[N\Sigma x^2) - (\Sigma x^2)]\ [N\Sigma y^2) - (\Sigma y^2)]}$$

Where,

r = coefficient of correlation
Σ= the summation
x = value of first variable
Y= Value of 2nd variables
N= total number of pairs

Multiple Regression Analysis

Multiple regression analysis method was used to find out the influence of independent variables on dependent variables:

The equation used was

$Y = a + b_1x_1 + B_2X_2$ .... b_nx_n

Where,

X_1 = Xn are the independent variable a is constant and

b_1 .... b_n regression weight for respective variables

This analysis was done to know the combine effect of all the independent variables in explaining the variation dependent variable.

The findings of the study are presented in the next chapter.

4

Result and Discussion

The findings of this study on tribal dairy co-operatives societies and their impact on the lives of tribal people were presented and discussed in this chapter under the following sections:

(I) Integrated Tribal Dairy Development Programme: Genesis, growth and achievements

(II) Socio-economic profile of respondents under study

(III) Differences between beneficiaries of ITDDP and non-beneficiaries

(IV) Impact of ITDDP on achievement target indicators and economic performance

(V) Opinion of tribal respondents and TDCS officials on the ITDDP activities.

(VI) Socio-economic changes in living standards of tribal people after the introduction of ITDDP

(VII) Factors affecting knowledge and adoption of improved dairy production technologies

milk production and sale of milk to dairy co-operatives.

(VIII) Problems faced by tribal farmer respondents and ITDDP officials

(IX) Members suggestions form smooth runnning of TDCSs

(X) Strategy of strengthening dairy development programme in tribal areas

Section I: Integrated Tribal Dairy Development Programme:Genesis, Growth and Achievement

Madhya Pradesh is the largest state in India endowed with largest cattle population in any state with more than 28 million cattle amounting to 14 per cent of total cattle population in India as per statistics available in 1992. This state has great production potential. But the procurements of milk from the cooperatives as per cent of production were a mere 1.66 compared to 6.58 at national level according to statistics available in 1998-99 (NDDB, 1998-99).

In 1990, a massive dairy development programme called Integrated Tribal Dairy Development Programme (ITDDP) was started in 10 selected tribal dominated districts of Madhya Pradesh. The ten districts were Bastar, Sarguja, Raigarh, Shahdol, Balaghat, Sidhi, Chindwara, Rajnadgam, Mandla and Jhabua. This programme was started under the Operation Flood with the collaboration of National Dairy Development Board (NDDB), Madhya Pradesh Adivasi Vitta Avam Vikas Nigam, National Scheduled Caste/

Scheduled Tribes Finance and Development cooperatives (NSFDC). Under the ITDDP, a network of Tribal Dairy cooperatives societies (TDCS) were formed at village level, and dairy unions at district level to coordinated and managed by Madhya Pradesh Dairy Cooperatives Federation Ltd., Bhopal (M.P).

Tribal Dairy Co-operative Societies (TDCS) were established at village level and managed by elected tribal milk producers. An institutional framework of co-operative structure at various levels had not only ensured a ready and regularly buyer of milk at guaranteed remunerative prices for tribal farmers but also helped link remote tribal villages with city and urban markets and ensured regular milk supply to urban customers.

Rationale

Tribal people were found to maintain medium to large livestock herds as these people perceive many advantages such as provision of milk thereby ensuring food and nutrition security, income generation, capital accumulation (due to regular calving), provision of draught power, nutrient transfer through cowdung and farm yard manure, risk aversion, etc. Some of the tribal people were also found to perceive that milk is nature's gift to calf and not meant for income generation through it sale. If such negative thoughts were prevented and intensified and market oriented livestock farming expanded and promoted, it would result in the alround development of tribal communities.

Tribal people mainly depend on forest for their livelihood. They get all their needs of food; fodder, fuel and medicinal herbs form forest. But large-scale deforestation affected adversely the tribal life and economy. Available cultivable land in the tribal belt appears to be minimal thereby forcing tribal people to resort to wage employment as agricultural labourers. In addition, in these backward areas, employment opportunities available to tribal people were also quite minimal. In such situation, tribal people usually resort to raising cattle to supplement their family food requirements and if possible to supplement their family incomes.

Animal husbandry and dairying is a multifarious activity in tribal community providing off-seasonal work, steady income and keep farmers and their family members engaged alround the year. But the standard of dairy production practices adopted in tribal villages was observed to be poor in general. Cattle are usually let free and they are forced to subsist on foraging in large areas of vacant community pasturelands.

The objectives of ITDDP were:

- To organise and run dairy development programmes through milk producer's co-operative on the pattern of Annual.
- To ascertain assumed and regular payment of remunerative price of milk to farmers through Dairy co-operative societies.
- To provide balanced and nutritive cattle feed to milk producers.

- To organise publicity and extension programme on fodder development programmes.
- To provide the facilities for artificial insemination for cattle breed improvement through dairy cooperatives.
- To provide necessary animal health care services to TDCS members.
- To increase milk production through cross-breeding and cattle improvement.
- To construct necessary infrastructure for district dairy development programme.
- To make available good quality pasteurized milk at reasonable prices to consumers.
- To provide opportunities for employment to youth through linking dairy development activities of the district.
- To make as many tribal people as possible, the members of dairy cooperative so that they avail maximum benefits mentioned above.

Programme and Activities

Under the ITDDP, a series of activities would be undertaken which are coordinated at three levels at village level Tribal Dairy Cooperative Societies (TDCS), at district level milk union and at state level MPDCF or Federation.

One of the major functions of the ITDDP was to organise farmer's groups or organisation. This is usually done through organising milk producers group or tribal dairy cooperative societies and continuously increasing its membership. Such as effort would result in increased involvement and participation of tribal people.

Second most important function of ITDDP is to organise assured milk collection alround the year for regularly and assured income to tribal milk producers at remunerative prices. Such as effort would save them from exploitation by private milk vendors.

Under the ITDDP, cooperatives were being organised at three levels at milk production level at in villages. Tribal Dairy Co-operative Societies (TDCS), where each member's milk is collected. At milk processing level at district headquarters - District Milk Producers' Cooperative Union, which organises the collection and processing of milk at the district level. At the state level, milk producers' cooperative federation coordinates the dairy development programme and balances the areas of milk surplus with those that have a deficit. NDDB at national level helps the state governments in organising the cooperative institutional framework and infrastructure with an aim to standardize the national milk production and marketing system.

ITDDP benefits the tribal population by

(a) Recognising the fact that rural producers' commodities usually are perishable and thus need strong marketing support

(b) Ensuring a better price to milk producers thereby providing a stimulus for growth

(c) Introducing new dairy production technology and ensuring that such technology is equally available to all member producers, avoiding class disparities, through a well-established infrastructure.

(d) Employing modern management techniques for effective monitoring and coordination of dairy development programme activities.

Activities of ITDDP

Organising Tribals. Tribal people were organised into cooperative called Tribal Dairy Co-operative Societies (TDCS). The policy makers at ITDDP saw cooperatives as the temple of rural development and hence the farmers of these tribal areas were organised. Any tribal farmers who years a milch animal and has surplus milk to sell can become a member of the TDCS by paying a membership fee and share capital of Rs 10 along with a entry fee of Rs.1. An executive governing body of 9 members including one chairman, one vice-chairman, and seven executive committee members manages this cooperative. All these nine executive members are honorary office bearers. A trained and paid secretary and one or two paid assistants assist this obeyed.

II. Improved breeds of milch animals were provided to the farmers under the IRDP scheme at 50 per cent subsidized loans. Crossbred cows of Holstein Freisian, Tharparkar, Gir and Jersey and distributed among the tribal beneficiaries. Thus IRDP was linked with the ITDDP.

III. Madhuvan. Madhuvan has been conceived as a satellite centre for demonstration of dairy production technology. Cattle shed were built and about 20 crosses bread jersey cows were provided. These cows were given to tribal beneficiaries but actually put in Madhuvans and are stall-fed and taken care of by the tribal people as well as the ITDDP officials including veterinary officers. The sale proceeds of the milk of these cows were given to tribals and also sent as installment of repayment of loans on a 50-50 basis. The 'Madhuvan' were functioning on the lives of modern dairy management.

Staff Pattern/Organisation

The ITDDP is managed by a project manager at district level under whom one milk procurement officer, one veterinary officer and fodder development officer work for milk procurement. Veterinary services and fodder development programmes.

Two field officers and about twelve village extension officers assist the milk procurement officer. The VEOs are dairy cooperative supervisors and supervise the functioning of the paid secretaries of each TDCS. VEO's are also responsible for milk procurement, transportation, sale to Union Dairy and payment of dues to TDCS, sale of cattle concentrate feed, supply of liquid nitrogen tanks for carrying semen for artificial insemination, supply and distribute fodder seeds to each TDCS. He also works for the maintenance of close links with the members of the TDCS, listen to their complaints and solve their problems He also checks the records of the TDCS maintained by the paid secretary of TDCS. He is also responsible for reporting. He prepares monthly progress and information reports and sends them to the project manager thro proper channels.

Under the ITDDP, the chief activities included are:

- To motivate farmers to take up dairy enterprise
- To distribute exotic/improved breeds of cows
- To provide training to farmers on scientific dairy production and management practices
- To improve local breeds of cows through artificial insemination
- To provide timely veterinary treatment to dairy animals
- To provide cattle feed mixtures for better animals nutrition
- To encourage fodder crop production through provision of fodder crop seed
- To provide assured market at tribal villages, and
- To improve the socio-economic condition of the tribal people

When the milk collection van goes to each village on its route, the secretary sends written requests form members for veterinary services, wherever members face any emergency. Within 4-8 hours, the veterinary surgeon comes on a motorcycle or jeep and provides necessary veterinary treatments and services.

Thus, the TDCSs under ITDDP were found to be patterned an Anand Model Dairy and are being run by the MPCDF and the state government of Madhya Pradesh.

Fig 4.1 Organisational set up of Madhya Pradesh Dairy Cooperative Federation (MPDCF)

State level MPDCF

Chairman

↓

Managing Director

↓

General Mangers

↓

Procurement
Farmers organisation
Veterinary services
Fodder developemnt
Marketing
Finance
Administration

District level Project officer/manager

Milk procurement officer ——— One
Field officer ——— Two
Veterinary officer ——— One

Fodder development officer ——— One
Village level Village Extension officers (VEO)- 12
TDCS
Chairman (1) Elected
Vice-chairman (1) Elected
Executive committee members (7) Elected body
Secretary - (1) Appointed and paid by TDCS
Assistant (1 or 2) - (1 & 2) Appointed & paid by TDCS

Fig. 4.2 State Government Machinery for Dairy Development

State level ——— Dairy commissioner

Division level ——— Depty dairy commissoner

District level ——— District dairy manager

Shift manager (one)
Manager chilling plant (one)
Dairy chemist (one)
Village level ———— Asstt.Village milk procurement

The TDCSs in each village is being run by a domocratically elected executive body of society's members. An educated youth of the village is usually be selected to work as a secretary, who maintains records, tests milk, collects milk and send its daily to the road by head form where milk collection van takes it away to district Milk Union's Chilling Centre. He is also responsible for weekly payments to members. Secretary to TDCS, who is a paid tribal farmer, get adequate training in record maintenance, first aid, artificial insemination, vaccination and milk testing. He is also responsible for proper cleaning of utensil; proper unkeep of the milk collection centre.

Tribal dairy cooperative societies at village level were assigned to perform a set of specific functions such as

(i) Collection of milk form individual members at appointed collection centres at appointed times

(ii) Testing of individual centres at appointed times

(iii) Transportation and sale of milk to the district milk producers cooperative union dairy

(iv) Payment of money to individual members according to the quantity and quality of milk supplied.

(v) Purchase of cattle feed, vaccines, medicines and their distribution and sale of the primary milk producers

(vi) Dealing with insurance companies and banks

(vii) Train the tribal milk producers an improved fodder production, stall-feeding and other significant dairy management practices

(viii) To organise and maintain records of milk collection and payment of annual bonus at members.

Section II: Socio-economic Profile of Respondents

As has already been presented in the chapter on 'Research methodology'. 20 beneficiary tribal farmers and 20 non-beneficiary tribal farmers from each of the five tribal districts were studied. Here an attempt was made to study the socio -economic profile of these respondents. The socio-economic characteristics of farmers studied are age, education, family type, family size, type of houses, livestock, herd size, annual family income, social participant, credit orientation, extension contact mass media exposure, knowledge of farmers on dairy production technology, extent of adoption of dairy production technology, opinion of farmers towards ITDDP, milk production and milk sale.

2.1 Age

Age of an individual is one of the factors that might influence his behaviour. The tribal farmers were classified into three categories viz., young (below 35 years), middle aged (36 to 50 years) and old (above 50 years). The data reveal that about 80 per cent of beneficiaries were below 50 years while more than 70 per cent of non-beneficiaries were above 50 years old. While the beneficiary respondents' distribution on their age appears to be normal, non-beneficiaries' distribution appears to be highly skewed towards old age.

2.2. Education

Education was found to be an important variable in the studies on adoption behaviour. Here the tribal farmer respondents were classified into ten groups on their level of formal education viz., illiterate, can read only, can read and write, having attended primary school or middle school or high school, having completed intermediate and having obtained a graduate degree or a post graduate degree and having obtained a diploma in a professional or vocational technical course. The data clearly indicated that the non-beneficiaries were distributed towards the illiteracy end of the spectrum with as many as 70 per cent respondents being barely able to read and write. But beneficiary respondents seem to be evenly distributed. About 46 per cent of the beneficiaries had higher level of education with nearly 25 per cent having had an education beyond intermediate level. This can e seen as a positive indicator of progressiveness and hence may have resulted in higher extent of adoption of dairy production technology.

2.3 Type of Family

Tribal people live in two types of family settings either in combined and extended joint families or in nuclear families. The data revealed that, about two-thirds of non-beneficiary tribal farmers preferred to live in nuclear families compared to a little a more than half of beneficiary farmers. Rearing cattle for dairying demands the use of family labour and preference of beneficiary farmers to live in joint families would help in the supply of adequate family labour.

2.4 Size of Family

Size of family plays an important role in tribal economy the more the better. The respondents were classified into three groups-one having a family size of upto 5 members, second having 6 to 8 family members and the third group having more than 9 family members. The data reveal that both the beneficiaries and non-beneficiary respondents prefer bigger families. But 50 per cent beneficiary farmers had medium size families while about the same number of non-beneficiaries had bigger size families

2.5 Housing

Type of house owned is an important symbol of standard of living one enjoys in society. In tribal societies also, the type of house indicates one's status in his village. The data reveal that the tribal farmers' housing condition is poor and highly skewed towards thatched and kaccha houses. About ninety-seven per cent of non-beneficiaries lived in such poor houses compared to about ninety-one per cent of beneficiaries. Beneficiary tribal farmers had more mixed houses than non-beneficiary farmers.

2.6 Material Possession

Materials including farm and domestic materials possessed by an individual also play an important role in tribal economy. A score of one each was given to each material possessed and the total score was computed. The respondents were classified into three groups of low material possession score (up to 5), medium score (6 to 10) and high score (11 and above). The data reveal that while the beneficiary tribal farmers were distributed normally on this variable of material possession, the non-beneficiary tribal farmers were highly skewed toward lower scores. About 60 per cent of non-beneficiaries had lower level of material possession while about the same number of beneficiaries had medium to higher level of material possession. About 33 per cent of beneficiaries had higher level of material possession compared to only 2 per cent of non-beneficiaries. This can be seen as a positive indicator of benefits getting accrued to the tribal people who were becoming members in tribal dairy cooperative societies and working for dairy development.Beneficiary tribal farmers showed a marked increase in their material possession over the non-beneficiary respondents especially in possession such items as chaff-cutter, cycle, scooter, radio, wooden almirah, chairs, tables sewing machine, etc.

2.7 Occupation

One's occupation is an important source of income. Among the tribals, though farming may be a primary occupation, hunting and collecting wood and other forest products also was being practiced.Both groups of respondents appear to be more or less equal in their number of people opting for a particular occupation, though there were slightly more agricultural labourers among non-beneficiaries and slightly more farmers among beneficiary respondents. Farming had become a main occupation among all the tribal farmer respondents.

2.8 Land Size

Land holding is again an important aspect of tribal economy. The respondents were classified in to seven groups ranging from landless to landlords. The data reveal that the both groups of respondents were more or less equally distributed among all the seven land size categories. They appear to be varying only on two categories-while non-beneficiaries were slightly more in the land size category of below one acre, the beneficiary respondents were slightly more in the land size category of 1 to 2.5 acres.

2.9 Herd Size

Cows and bullocks are the most important livestock in tribal culture. The cattle are usually set free and move around grazing freely on the forest pasturelands. These tribal respondents usually possess more number of cattle. These respondents were classified into four groups, viz., are having 1-2 animals for animal husbandry, are having 3 to 5 animals, or having 6 - 9 animals and lastly, are having more than 10 animals The data indicate that the livestock herd size was normally distributed among the beneficiary respondents while it was observed to be slightly skewed towards lesser number of cattle among non-beneficiaries. The beneficiary farmers, who were the members of tribal dairy cooperative societies, possessed varying number of cattle. Big dairy farmers, having more than 10 animals were also members in the tribal dairy cooperative society along with small dairy farmers having only one or two dairy animals. It appears from the table that the membership of tribal dairy cooperative societies was open to all types of farmers irrespective of their herd size. Participation of all size categories of farmers in the dairy development programme was observed.

2.10 Annual Family Income

Annual family income is an important factor that might is affecting the participation of tribal farmer respondents in dairy development programmes. The respondents were classified into eight groups based on their income with the first group of respondents having an increase of less than Rs. 10, 000 and subsequent seven groups with an incremental income of Rs. 5000 over the previous group. The data reveal two differently skewed distributions. While the distribution of non-beneficiaries was found to be highly skewed towards lower annual family income, beneficiaries' distribution was more or less even. While nearly eighty per cent non-beneficiaries earned incomes upto Rs. 30,000, only 50 per cent beneficiaries did so. More than 20 per cent of beneficiaries were found to earn annual family incomes more than Rs. 40,000. Beneficiaries were getting more annual family income than the non-beneficiaries.

2.11 Social Participation

Tribal farmers' participation in social organisations might have an influence on their participation in tribal dairy development programmes. The respondents were classified into three groups on the basis of the range of scores as low, moderate and high level of social participation

The data clearly reveal that the beneficiary tribal farmers were participating actively in various social organisations including the tribal dairy cooperative society. With high level of participation scores, nearly 40 per cent were also found to be office bearers of these social organisations. But about 85 per cent non-beneficiary tribal farmers' level of social participation was low. Both the distributions were found to be representatively skewed towards higher level of social participation of beneficiaries and towards low level of social participation of non-beneficiaries.

The data in the table reveals that the local moneylender is the one single source used mostly by non-beneficiary respondents and also by beneficiary tribal farmers. But beneficiaries were moving towards institutional sources of finance in more numbers than the non-beneficiaries. Primary cooperative credit societies and bank appeared to be getting popular among the tribal people.

Some of the tribal farmer respondents in the beneficiaries' category were found to be actively participating in social institution not only at village level bat also at black and district level. Some were found to be either retired office bearers of one organization but actively participating in the affairs of more than one social organization, says Gram Panchayat, Tribal Dairy Cooperative Society or even in political organisations. One or two respondents were also enjoying the status of a public leader with great mass appeal.

2.12 Credit Orientation

Credit is an important factor in the lives of tribal people whose annual family incomes were very less and families bigger. Tribal farmer respondents were classified into four groups on the basis of their sources of credit local moneylender, primary cooperative credit societies or banks, neighbours and relatives and last those who did not take any loan.

The data reveal that the local moneylender is the one single source used mostly by non-beneficiary respondent and also by beneficiary tribal farmers. But beneficiaries were moving towards institutional sources of finance in more members than the non-beneficiaries. Primary cooperative credit societies and bank appeared to be getting popular among the tribal people.

4.2.13 Extension Contact

Contacting extension agencies for farm advisory services is an important factor contributing to the adoption of improved dairy production technologies by the tribal farmers with the introduction of ITDDP in these tribal villages, farmers were found to be frequently interacting with many government officers like livestock assistant, veterinary assistant surgeon, Agricultural officers, minor forest produce officers in addition to meeting the trained secretary of their own society in their village. Tribal dairy cooperative society. The scores for each respondent's farmers were calculated on the basis of the scores discussed in the Methodology chapter. Then the scores were categorised into three groups - low with a score of 0-8, with a score ranging from 9 to 16 and high frequency of extent contact with a score ranging from 17 to 25. The data for both categories of respondents is presented in Table 4.2.1.

The data in the table clearly bring two focuses that the non-beneficiaries' frequency of contact was very low in nearly 80 per cent of tribal farmers. On the other hand about 85 per cent of beneficiaries were found to be contacting extension agencies very frequently-from moderate to high.Both the distribution were found to be highly skewed-while non-beneficiaries' distribution was skewed towards the low frequency level, beneficiaries' distribution was skewed towards high level of frequency of extension agency contact.

Table 4.2.1 Distribution of Respondents on Extension Contact

Source of credit	*Beneficiaries (N=100)*	*Non-beneficiaries (N=100)*
Low (0-8)	15	79
Moderate (9-16)	47	13
High (17-25)	38	08

4.2.14 Mass Media Exposure

Exposure to mass media is another important factor contributing to the awareness of individuals. Here the frequency of exposure of tribal farmers to mass media like radio, television, newspaper, literature, exhibition, etc. was studied using the scale developed for the purpose. The total scores were categorized into three groups of low exposure; moderate exposure and high level of exposure to mass media and the data were presented in Table 4.2.2.

The data presented din the table reveals that the beneficiaries and non-beneficiaries were quite different from each other in mass media exposure. While 85 per cent of non-beneficiaries had low exposure, 96 per cent of beneficiaries had moderate to high level of mass media exposure. The frequency distributions were also found to be highly skewed in both categories of respondents on mass media exposure. The high mass media exposure of beneficiaries may have been due to their high social participation and higher social status.

Table 4.2.2 Distribution of Respondents on Mass Media Exposure

Mass media exposure category	*Beneficiaries (N=100)*	*Non-beneficiaries (N=100)*
Low (0-8)	04	85
Moderate (9-16)	45	15
High (17-26)	51	0

4.2.15 Knowledge of Dairy Production Technologies

Under the ITDDP, the tribal farmers were given critical exposure to improved dairy production technologies, including providing veterinary services like artificial insemination of cows, better feeding practices, fodder production, health care and treatment of sick animals, and better dairy management. These services are provided through trained secretary of TDCS, visiting livestock assistants, veterinary surgeons and project officers of ITDDP. Here an attempt has been made to measure the knowledge level of tribal farmers through a knowledge test developed for the study.

The knowledge test contained 24 items including seven items on breeding practices, five items on healthy care and 6 items each on dairy management and animal nutrition an fodder crop production. The tribal farmers respondents knowledge was tested and the total scores were categorised into three groups low, medium and high level of knowledge. The data for both categories of respondents is presented in Table 4.2.3.

The data presented in the table reveals that the frequency distribution of non-beneficiaries was highly skewed forward low level of knowledge. On the other hand, the distribution of beneficiaries was highly skewed towards high level of knowledge. More than ninety per cent of beneficiaries had medium to high level of knowledge of dairy production technologies.

Table 4.2.3 Distribution of Respondents on Knowledge of Dairy Production Technologies

Level of Knowledge	*Beneficiaries*	*Non- beneficiaries*
Low (0-8)	08	49
Medium (9-16)	38	50
High (> 17)	54	01

4.2.4 Extent of Adoption of Dairy Production Technologies

The extent to which a tribal dairy farmers respondents adopts improved dairy production technologies is an important aspect to the success of the dairy development programme inn the tribal districts. To study the variable, a schedule was developed to include 24 items, which addressed four-sub topics breeding, feeding, health care and dairy management. Total scores for each respondent was calculated and the scores were categorised into three groups - low medium and high. The data are presented in Table 4.2.4.

Table 4.2.4 Distribution of Extent of Adoption of Dairy Production Technologies

Extent of adoption	*Beneficiaries (N=100)*	*Non-beneficiaries (N=100)*
Low (0-8)	08	49
Medium (9-16)	38	50
High (> 17)	54	01

The data presented in the table clearly shows that extent of adoption of improved dairy production technologies among the beneficiaries was found to be ranging from moderate to high and the frequency distribution appears to be normal. But the non-beneficiaries' distribution of respondents on extent of adoption was highly skewed towards the lower end of the continuum.

4.2.17 Milk Production

The total milk produced in the dairy unit of each tribal farmers respondents was recorded and data are presented in Table 4.2.5. It appears from the table that more than 90 per cent beneficiary respondents were selling more than three litres of milk each day to TDCS. There appears to be a consistent flow of milk at milk collection centres

Table 4.2.5 Total Milk Production by each Tribal Farmers Respondents

Milk in (litres)	*Beneficiaries (N=100)*	*Non-beneficiarie (N=100)*
1-5	13	42
6-10	34	41
11-15	24	09
16-20	19	06
21-25	10	02

and to district milk union. Even the non-beneficiaries were also found to sell milk to TDCS, through only about 14 per cent. It is also clear form the data presented in the two tables given above that the tribal dairy farmers appear to sell milk to private milk vendors in large quantities and barely patronizing the TDCS with an average of only 3 litres per day by each member. Some of the variables were not addressed in this section on profile of respondents. These were discussed in greater detail in separated section in the chapter.

Thus the average profile of respondents can be drawn as thus; Beneficiary tribal dairy farmer respondents appear to middle aged, educated up to middle school level, living in a nuclear family with medium size of family in a kachha house and possessing more than six items of far equipment and household goods. The average beneficiary farmers had farming and dairying as the principal occupation, possessing about six acres of land on an average with cattle herd size of six animals on his farm, and earning an average annual farming income of about Rs. 30000 only. He appears to be actively participating in more than one social organisation both at village and block level and usually taking loans from local moneylenders in the village.

The data presented in the table reveals that the total milk production by the tribal farmers respondents ranged from 1-25 litres. While about 47 per cent of beneficiaries were producing less than 10 liters of milk per day, about 83 per cent of non-beneficiaries were doing so. About 40 per cent beneficiary respondents were found to produce milk ranging from 11 to 20 litres per day per dairy unit. It appears that the milk production in the flush season (during which the data was collected by the researchers) is good amount.

4.2.18 Milk Sale

The amount of milk sold by the respondent households to the tribal dairy cooperative society (on the day prior to the investigation) was recorded and the data are presented in Table 4.2.6.

In moderately high frequency of contact with extension agencies and having better than medium level of exposure to mass media. He was found to possess moderate level of knowledge and so also had moderate extent of adoption of dairy production technologies. Though the produces more than 9 litres of milk as on average, he was found to sell 3 litres of milk only to TDCS in his village.

On the contrary, the non-beneficiary tribal dairy farmer respondent appear to be old in age, educated upto primary school level, living in a nuclear family with large size of family in a kachha house and possessing less than five items of farm equipments and household goods. The average non-beneficiary farmers had farming and dairying as the primary occupation, possessing about five acres of land on an average with cattle herd size of four animals on his farm, and earning an average annual family income of about Rs. 25000 only. The non-beneficiary tribal farmers appear to be not actively participating in any social organisations of the villages and usually taking loans from village moneylenders. He appears to have a low frequency of contact with extension

Table 4.2.6 Total Milk Sold by the Respondents to TDCS

Milk in (litres)	*Beneficiaries (N=100)*	*Non-beneficiarie (N=100)*
0	04	86
1	0	05
2	04	02
3	88	07
4and above	04	0

agents, and less exposure to mass media. His knowledge of improved diary production technologies was also very low and hence lowers extent of adoption. Though he produces about 7 litres of milk per day on a average, he hardly sells any to TDCS but selling elsewhere or consuming in their large families.

In the end, the data including means and standard deviation of all the variables was computed and presented. In this table, the data on beneficiaries, non-beneficiaries and pooled samples all participants is presented to enable a comparison of the variables.

Table 4.3.1: Difference between Beneficiaries and Non- beneficiaries on Socio-economic, Socio-psychological and Communicational Characteristics

S.No	*Variables*	*Beneficiaries*	*Non-beneficiaries*	*Difference*	*'t' value*
1.	Age ***	41.55	55.00	-13.45	-9.78 *
2.	Education ***	4.69	1.21	3.48	14.04 *
3.	Family type	1.46	1.34	0.12	1.74
4.	Family size	7.81	8.33	-0.52	-1.68
5.	Housing **	1.96	1.75	0.21	2.78
6.	Material possession ***	9.10	4.84	4.26	8.65
7.	Occupation	2.99	2.91	0.08	0.58

(Contd.)

(Contd. Table 4.3.1)

S.No	Variables	Beneficiaries	Non-beneficiaries	Difference	't' value
8.	Farm size	5.922	5.48	0.43	0.64
9.	Herd size ***	5.910	4.50	1.41	3.96
10.	Annual family income ***	5.980	4.01	1.86	3.84
11.	Social participation ***	13.18	4.66	8.52	21.16
12.	Credit orientation ***	1.42	1.73	0.29	4.47
13.	Extension contact ***	14.74	5.12	9.62	18.69
14.	Mass media exposure ***	16.20	5.38	10.82	20.55
15.	Knowledge of DPT ***	16.34	8.02	8.32	13.66

(Contd.)

(Contd. Table 4.3.1)

S.No	*Variables*	*Beneficiaries*	*Non-beneficiaries*	*Difference*	*'t' value*
16.	Adoption of DPT ***	12.87	5.79	5.75	9.22
17.	Opinion towards ***	13.01	4.07	8.94	19.32
18.	Milk production ***	12.00	7.18	4.82	6.50
19.	Milk sale ***	2.96	0.30	2.66	21.41

't' value at 198 degrees of freedom at 0.05 level of significance = 1.960
0.01 (0.01) = 2.576
0.01 (0.001) = 3.291

Section III: Differences between Beneficiaries of ITDDP and Non-beneficiaries

In the previous section on the profile of respondents, it has been reported that the beneficiaries and non-beneficiaries were distributed differently on many of the socio-personal variables. In this section an attempt has been made to find out the number of variables on which these two categories of respondents significantly vary. The mean difference on these variables was compared using a paired "t" test and the results are presented in the table 4.3.1.

As can be seen from the table, out of the nineteen variables under study, the beneficiaries of ITDDP and the non-beneficiaries were significantly different on fifteen variables. The four variables on which there were no differences between these two categories of respondents were family type, family size, land size and occupation. as has been reported in the previous section, the general description of all the respondents include that the tribal people in general live in joint families with large family size of more than seven

family members. They were also found to be possessing on an average 5 acres of land with primary occupation being farming.

Socio-personal Characteristics

The beneficiaries tribal farmer respondents were found to be significantly different from non-beneficiary tribal farmer respondents on age, level of education, type of housing, material possession, herd size, annual family income social participation and credit orientation. The beneficiary respondents were found to be younger, more educated, having better type of housing, possessing larger herd size more domestic and farm and domestic materials, having higher degree of social participation, earning more income and having a high credit orientation than the non-beneficiary respondents.

Communication Variables

The beneficiaries' tribal farmer respondents were also found to be different from their fellow tribal farmers who were non-beneficiaries on the communication variables also. The mean differences on these two variables-extension contact and mass media exposure were found to be significant at 0.001 level of probability. This means that the beneficiaries had more and frequent contacts with extension officials including TDCS officials, veterinary surgeons, extension workers etc., than the non-beneficiaries. Similarly, the beneficiaries were also found to be exposed more and quite often to mass media like radio, newspaper, television and others than the non-beneficiaries respondents.

Knowledge and Adoption of Dairy Production Technology

The beneficiary tribal farmers being members of the tribal dairy cooperative societies get frequently in touch with dairy development officials and learn move about the dairy production technologies and also adopt improved dairy production technologies. This fact was clearly reflected in the higher mean differences of beneficiaries on the scores of level of knowledge and extent of adoption of dairy production technologies.

Opinion Towards ITDDP

This variable is the most significant of all the socio-personal variables which has marked fourth highest mean difference between the beneficiaries and non-beneficiaries and which may be influencing the acquisition of knowledge and promotion of adoption of improved dairy production technologies among the beneficiaries. The non-beneficiaries were found to be quite less favourable towards ITDDP activities.

Milk Production and Milk Sale to TDCS

Total milk production and total amount of milk sold to tribal dairy cooperatives society were also found to be significant different between the beneficiaries and non-beneficiaries.

Thus there were found to be six variables on which the mean difference between beneficiaries of ITDDP and non-beneficiaries were very high. These variables were age, mass media exposure, extension contact, and opinion towards ITDDP, social participation and the knowledge of dairy production technologies. The mean differences for these six variables ranged from -13.45 to 8.32.

At the outset, the discussion presented in the two sections II and III, it has been found that the beneficiary tribal farmers were significant better than the non-beneficiary tribal farmers.

Section IV: Impact of ITDDP an Achievement Target Indicators and Economic Performance

An attempt has been made in this section to analyses and discusses the possible impact of Integrated Tribal Dairy Development Program (ITDDP) on the dairy development in the tribal villages. Achievement target indicators have been measured and studied. They are (a) herd mortality indicators (i) herd mortality (ii) female calf mortality (iii) vaccination rate and (iv) veterinary treatment rate, (b) Breeding practices (i) breeding rate, (ii) pregnancy rate, (c) breeding behaviour indictors - (i) age at first calving, (ii) inter-calving period and (d) nutritional standard of the herd indictors i) sale of concentrate cattle feed ii) supply of fodder seed and iii) grazing land available.

These eleven achievement target indicators were analysis for each TDCS and the trends were also seen through rate of change over the three years period of 1996-97 to 1998-99.

Economic performance indictors included total members, total milk sellers, milk procurement and net profit made by each TDCS. These indictors were also analysed and discussed.

In all, twenty five TDCS, five each in five districts of Bastar, Mandla, Surguja, Raigarh and Jhabua were studied in this section to discern the impact of ITDDP on the dairy development activities and dairy cooperative performance among the tribal villages.

Achievement Target Indicators

Target area a set of concrete and quantifiable aims that have to be achieved by the Integrated Tribal Dairy Development Board (ITDDP). Indicators are numerical expression of the variables that explaining the relationship between as aim and its realisation.

For the purpose of this study, a set of target indictors have been studied which have been put into four broad groups. They are a) herd mortality, b) breeding practices c) breeding behaviour and d) nutritional standard of the herd.

The data on these four groups of indictors were calculated using the formulae already presented in the section III-variables and their measurement in Chapter III on "Research Methodology" and the data are presented in Table through and discussed in the following pages.

The data for each indictor was computed form the data collected from the secondary sources- the records maintained by each of the Tribal Dairy Cooperatives Society. The data were collected for three years-1996-97, 1997-98 and for 1998-99. For most of the indictors the data were available for three years. For a few variables, the data were available for only one year, 1996-97.

In cases, where the data were available in society records for three years, new data were generated on the rate of change over the years by using the formula:

$$\text{Rate of change in percentage} = \frac{(\text{Data of 1998-99}) - (\text{Data of 1996-97})}{(\text{Data of 1996-97})} \times 100$$

Thus the rate of charge in percentage was calculated for the target indicators, and is presented in the following tables.

Whereas, data were not available, the rate of percentage was not calculated. Then the data for the year 1996-97 were presented in the tables, and details were discussed.

(a) Herd Mortality

It has already been noted that the tribal people usually maintained large herds of cattle. But the health of the cattle is of great concern for the tribal farmer as it directly affects the herd build up in the long run and thereby the sustainability of dairying as enterprise. Four target indicators were studied under this group. Mortality rate, female calf mortality rate, vaccination rate and veterinary treatment rate. The last two indicators were included here because they play a crucial role in maintaining the health of the livestock and in reducing mortality.

Here, the data were available for all the three years for all the variables except for one indicators-vaccination rate for ten villages in two districts only. Vaccination was stopped after the year 1996-97 and so rate of change could not be calculated.

Mortality Rate

This target indicator is a proportion of dead animals to the total stock including the new animals added in a year. If new animals regularly replace the dead animals, the herd size will be maintained well. If this replacement were not taking place, herd mortality would have an adverse effect on the herd size and health, and ultimately on the productivity of the herd. The data pertaining to the target indicator are presented in the Table 4.4.1. .

Herd mortality as can be seen from the table, was found to be increasing rather than decreasing, over the three years period. Among the twenty-five villages studied, the mortality rate in the five vilalges each of Bastar and Jhabua was found to be lower with a maximum of 59 per 1000 in the year 1998-99. In the previous years, the mortality rate was much lower, as low a mortality rate as 26 per 1000. In Gopalpura of Jhabua, the mortality rate was found to be reducing at a rate of 9 per cent.

But in the village Mandla, Surguja and Raigarh, the mortality rates were very high with an average mortality rate of more than 70 per 1000 in the years 1998-99. The reason for much high mortality rates were many and will be discussed at length after a thorough analysis of all the four target indicators grouped under herd mortality indicators. The high mortality rates were really disturbing as the animal health services were found to be deteriorating in these villages.

Table 4. 4.1: Mortality Rate

S.No	*Year TDCS*	*1996-97*	*1997-98*	*1998-99*	*Rate of change in percentage*
Basrter					
1.	Tukaja wali	0.0362	0.0384	0.0463	27.90
2.	Korenar	0.0261	0.0389	0.0516	97.70
3.	Konargaon	0.0432	0.0529	0.0592	37.03
4.	Chogenmulla	0.0278	0.0320	0.0492	28.13
5.	Karamar	0.0384	0.0320	0.0492	28.13
	Average	0.03434	0.0389	0.05064	

(Contd.)

(Contd. Table 4.4.1)

S.No	Year TDCS	1996-97	1997-98	1998-99	Rate of change in percentage
Mandla					
6.	Babli	0.0538	0.0647	0.0784	45.72
7.	Khari	0.0495	0.0589	0.0674	36.16
8.	Khanderi	0.0525	0.0535	0.0742	41.33
9.	Bhilai	0.0328	0.0423	0.0486	48.17
10.	Bhapsa	0.0395	0.0510	0.0690	74.59
	Average	0.04562	0.05402	0.06752	

(Contd.)

(Contd. Table 4.4.1)

S.No	*Year TDCS*	*1996-97*	*1997-98*	*1998-99*	*Rate of change in percentage*
Surguja					
11.	Pampapur	0.0382	0.0480	0.0620	62.30
12.	Sonpur	0.0489	0.0670	0.0690	41.10
13.	Kailashpur	0.0321	0.0582	0.0702	118.69
14.	Silfili	0.0439	0.0639	0.0825	87.93
15.	Madluvan	0.0890	0.0982	0.1002	12.58
	Average	0.05042	0.06906	0.07678	

(Contd.)

(Contd. Table 4.4.1)

S.No	Year TDCS	1996-97	1997-98	1998-99	Rate of change in percentage
Raigarh					
16.	Basanpali	0.0429	0.0529	0.0632	47.31
17.	Pata	0.0538	0.0639	0.0640	18.96
18.	Jamura	0.0502	0.0589	0.0599	19.32
19.	Raniguda	0.0478	0.0580	0.0610	27.62
20.	Barpali	0.0521	0.0625	0.0690	32.64
	Average	0.04936	0.05924	0.06342	

(Contd.)

(Contd. Table 4.4.1)

S.No	*Year TDCS*	*1996-97*	*1997-98*	*1998-99*	*Rate of change in percentage*
Jhabua					
21.	Gopalpur	0.0528	0.0525	0.0480	9.0
22.	Tarkhedi	0.0482	0.0510	0.0590	22.41
23.	Chhayan	0.0475	0.0490	0.0535	11.00
24.	Jhadki	0.0328	0.0390	0.0410	25.00
25.	Jharadabarr	0.0296	0.0390	0.0450	52.02
	Average	0.4218	0.0461	0.0493	

Table 4.4.2: Female Calf-Mortality Rate

S.No	Year TDCS	1996-97	1997-98	1998-99	Rate of change in percentage
Baster					
1.	Tukaja wali	0.0825	0.1087	0.1127	36.61
2.	Korenar	0.0950	0.1120	0.1250	31.58
3.	Konargaon	0.0875	0.096	0.1025	17.14
4.	Chogenmulla	0.0990	0.1082	0.1150	16.16
5.	Karamar	0.0880	0.1140	0.1210	37.50
	Average	0.0904	0.10778	0.11524	

(Contd.)

(Contd. Table 4.4.2)

S.No	*Year TDCS*	*1996-97*	*1997-98*	*1998-99*	*Rate of change in percentage*
Mandla					
6.	Babli	0.0987	0.1210	0.1280	29.69
7.	Khari	0.0860	0.1179	0.1289	49.88
8.	Khanderi	0.0901	0.1021	0.1185	31.52
9.	Bhilai	0.0871	0.14041	0.1260	44.66
10.	Bhapsa	0.0960	0.1020	0.1199	24.90
	Average	0.09158	0.116802	0.12426	

(Contd.)

(Contd. Table 4.4.2)

S.No	Year TDCS	1996-97	1997-98	1998-99	Rate of change in percentage
Surguja					
11.	Pampapur	0.1028	0.1080	0.1280	24.52
12.	Sonpur	0.0918	0.1020	0.1235	34.53
13.	Kailashpur	0.0791	0.0999	0.1028	29.96
14.	Silfili	0.0982	0.1089	0.1175	19.65
15.	Madluvan	0.1036	0.1269	0.1380	33.20
	Average	0.0951	0.10914	0.12196	

(Contd.)

(Contd. Table 4.4.2)

S.No	*Year TDCS*	*1996-97*	*1997-98*	*1998-99*	*Rate of change in percentage*
Raigarh					
16.	Basanpali	0.0821	0.0997	0.1156	40.80
17.	Pata	0.0982	0.1045	0.1180	20.16
18.	Jamura	0.0865	0.1027	0.1186	37.16
19.	Raniguda	0.0988	0.1087	0.1115	12.85
20.	Barpali	0.0896	0.1031	0.1089	21.54
	Average	0.09104	0.10374	0.114552	

(Contd.)

(Contd.Table 4.4.2)

S.No	*Year TDCS*	*1996-97*	*1997-98*	*1998-99*	*Rate of change in percentage*
Jhabua					
21.	Gopalpur	0.0789	0.0993	0.1016	28.77
22.	Tarkhedi	0.0935	0.0982	0.1146	22.57
23.	Chhayan	0.0986	0.1038	0.1235	25.25
24.	Jhadki	0.0977	0.1100	0.1196	22.42
25.	Jharadabarr	0.0924	0.1084	0.1139	23.27
	Average	0.09222	0.10334	0.11464	

Female Calf Mortality Rate

This target indicator is a ratio of female calves dead to the opening stock plus new calves borne or brought into the cooperative during this year. Female calf is usually considered an asset that directly affects the success of the dairy enterprise and the death of female calf adversely affects the milk production in future. The data related to female calf mortality rate was available for the three years and rate of changes was also calculated. These data are presented in Table 4.4.2.

The data presented in the table reveals a very alarming scenario of the tribal dairy cooperative societies progress. The female calf mortality rate was found to be increasing over the three years period in all the villages of all the districts under study. The average female calf mortality rate was found to be range from 90/1000 to 120/1000 in these villages.

The rate of changes (increase) of female calf mortality rate was found to vary from 13 per cent to 50 per cent in the villages under study. This implies that female calf mortality rate instead of reducing was rather increasing adversely affecting the success and sustainability of dairying among the tribal community.

Vaccination Rate

Vaccinating the livestock was recommended as a necessary practices to maintain the health of the herd and to prevent any attack of epidemic diseases like foot and mouth disease, Haemerogic scepticemia and black quarter (HSBQ) etc. Vaccinate rate is the number of vaccinations injected as a proportion of the total number of cattle. This target indicator implicity assumes that an increase in the vaccination rate will lead to a fall in the mortality rates, especially with respect to female calf-mortality.

Vaccinations were done in all the villages till 1996-97. But in the years 1997-98 and 1998-99, was vaccinations were done in ten villagesunder study, those of Bastar and Mandla. The rate of change was calculated wherever possible. The data pertaining to these indicators are presented in Table 4.4.3.

The data presented in the table reveal that in the year 1996-97, large campaigns of vaccination were organised in these five districts under study. In these campaigns, as many as 750/1000 animals were vaccinated an average in the district Jhabua with the lowest average per district was with the district of Mandla at 424/1000 animals under each tribal dairy succeeding years, the picture was quite different. In two districts, vaccination was not done at all. But in the other three districts, the efforts were cold to lukewarm with an average vaccination rate of about 200/1000. This deterioration of health service was found to be affecting the herd mortality rates as was already seen in the previous tables of data.

Table 4. 4.3: Vaccination Rate

S.No	*Year TDCS*	*1996-97*	*1997-98*	*1998-99*	*Rate of change in percentage*
Basrter					
1.	Tukaja wali	0.5012	0.00	0.00	-
2.	Korenar	0.4162	0.00	0.00	-
3.	Konargaon	0.6216	0.00	0.00	-
4.	Chogenmulla	0.7580	0.00	0.00	-
5.	Karamar	0.6280	0.00	0.00	-
	Average	0.585	0.00	0.00	

(Contd.)

(Contd.Table 4.4.3)

S.No	*Year TDCS*	*1996-97*	*1997-98*	*1998-99*	*Rate of change in percentage*
Mandla					
6.	Babli	0.3820	0.00	0.00	-
7.	Khari	0.3680	0.00	0.00	-
8.	Khanderi	0.4800	0.00	0.00	-
9.	Bhilai	0.3900	0.00	0.00	-
10.	Bhapsa	0.5010	0.00	0.00	-
	Average	0.424	0.00	0.00	

(Contd.)

(Contd. Table 4.4.3)

S.No	*Year TDCS*	*1996-97*	*1997-98*	*1998-99*	*Rate of change in percentage*
Surguja					
11.	Pampapur	0.6120	0.00	0.1025	-83.25
12.	Sonpur	0.5800	0.2010	0.00	-65.34
13.	Kailashpur	0.5100	0.00	0.2510	-50.78
14.	Silfili	0.5750	0.1580	0.928	-72.52
15.	Madluvan	0.7710	0.0821	0.00	-89.35
	Average	0.6096	0.08822	0.2563	

(Contd.)

(Contd. Table 4.4.3)

S.No	*Year TDCS*	*1996-97*	*1997-98*	*1998-99*	*Rate of change in percentage*
Raigarh					
16.	Basanpali	0.612	0.00	0.1510	-75.33
17.	Pata	0.5210	0.3510	0.1510	-71.02
18.	Jamura	0.6210	0.1829	0.1829	-70.55
19.	Raniguda	0.6810	0.2080	0.1290	-81.06
20.	Barpali	0.6580	0.1020	0.1480	-77.51
	Average	0.6186	0.16878	0.16458	

(Contd)

(Contd. Table 4.4.3)

S.No	Year TDCS	1996-97	1997-98	1998-99	Rate of change in percentage
Jhabua					
21.	Gopalpur	0.8120	0.0820	0.2690	-66.87
22.	Tarkhedi	0.7810	0.3580	0.4050	-48.14
23.	Chhayan	0.6580	0.3210	0.2510	-61.19
24.	Jhadki	0.7510	0.2580	0.3687	-50.91
25.	Jharadabarr	0.7680	0.3010	0.3278	-57.32
	Average	0.754	0.304	0.3243	

Veterinary Treatment Rate. Treating the animals at the right time was an important aspects of maintaining the health of the herd. The target indictor-veterinary treatment rate is the number of veterinary treatments given in a year as a proportion of the total number of cattle at the end of the year. The data pertaining to this indictor were presented in table Table 4.4.4.

The data presented in the table reveal some interesting observations. First, a comparison of data over the three years period shows that the initial enthusiasm shown by tribal farmers respondents for veterinary treatment of the veterinary doctors was found to vane off soon just after 1996-97. Another interesting aspects was that only Jhabua could maintain continuous treatment of their animals in all the villages under study and for all the three years.

(b) Breeding Practices

This set of target indictors' deal with the various breeding practices undertaken by the trained paid secretary of Tribal Dairy Cooperative Societies, the visiting veterinary doctors, etc. to improve their breeding behaviour of herd and to reduce the number of dry animals in the herd. These practices include regular heat detection, insemination and pregnancy detection of the animals in the herd. These activities were evaluated with the help of a set of target indicators, viz.,

Table 4. 4.4: Veterniary Treatment Rate

S.No	*Year TDCS*	*1996-97*	*1997-98*	*1998-99*	*Rate of change in percentage*
Bastar					
1.	Tukaja wali	0.7208	0.2010	0.1580	-78.07
2.	Korenar	0.7129	0.2180	0.1230	-87.74
3.	Konargaon	0.6216	0.1860	0.1090	-82.43
4.	Chogenmulla	0.8420	0.1274	0.0987	-88.28
5.	Karamar	0.7880	0.01038	0.0876	-88.89
	Average	0.73706	0.16724	0.11526	

(Contd.)

(Contd. Table 4.4.4)

S.No	Year TDCS	1996-97	1997-98	1998-99	Rate of change in percentage
Mandla					
6.	Babli	0.6125	0.1021	0.0765	-87.51
7.	Khari	0.5890	0.0910	0.0864	-85.53
8.	Khandehi	0.5910	0.0980	0.0434	-92.66
9.	Bhilai	0.6325	0.1034	0.0587	-90.71
10.	Bhapsa	0.6485	0.0869	0.0657	-89.87
	Average	0.6147	0.09626	0.6614	

(Contd.)

(Contd.Table 4.4.4)

S.No	*Year TDCS*	*1996-97*	*1997-98*	*1998-99*	*Rate of change in percentage*
Surguja					
11.	Pampapur	0.5895	0.0569	0.0231	-96.08
12.	Sonpur	0.6635	0.0248	0.0358	-94.60
13.	Kailashpur	0.6970	0.0924	0.0825	-88.16
14.	Silfili	0.7810	0.0826	0.0652	-91.65
15.	Madluvan	0.8810	0.0210	0.0110	-98.75
	Average	0.7724	0.05554	0.0431	

(Contd.)

(Contd.Table 4.4.4)

S.No	*Year TDCS*	*1996-97*	*1997-98*	*1998-99*	*Rate of change in percentage*
Raigarh					
16.	Basanpali	0.8710	0.2180	0.1520	-82.54
17.	Pata	0.8890	0.1820	0.1080	-87.85
18.	Jamura	0.7765	0.2169	0.0580	-92.53
19.	Raniguda	0.9085	0.2810	0.1128	-88.10
20.	Barpali	0.8981	0.1896	0.0980	-89.08
	Average	0.86862	0.2175	0.10576	

(Contd)

(Contd. Table 4.4.4)

S.No	Year TDCS	1996-97	1997-98	1998-99	Rate of change in percentage
Jhabua					
21.	Gopalpur	0.9610	0.3510	0.4810	-30.39
22.	Tarkhedi	0.7123	0.4868	0.5880	-17.55
23.	Chhayan	0.8340	0.6820	0.6670	-19.24
24.	Jhadki	0.8681	0.7030	0.7120	-17.98
25.	Jharadabarr	0.9191	0.7280	0.6887	-25.07
	Average	0.8049	0.599016	0.62734	

breeding rate and pregnancy rate which reflects directly the efficiency of otherwise for the trained staff of TDCS in performing these activities and indirectly, the breeding behaviour of the herd.

Breeding Rate

This refers to the ratio of inseminated cattle to the non-pregnant cattle. It influences not only the milk yield in the short-run, but also the future herd build-up. It also helps in monitoring the efficiency of trained secretary of TDCS in detecting animals in heat and facilitating their timely insemination. The data for these indicators are presented in Table 4.4.5

A cursory look at the data in the table reveals a declining trend in the breeding rate in all the 25 TDCS. In Bastar, Mandla and Surguja, the breeding rate decline was very sharp and faster. In Raigah the declining trend was not so sharply seen. Only in Jhabua, there was a marginal decline in the rate of change. These declining trends of breeding rates imply a disturbing future scenario, as the herd's long-term build up was not taken care of. The heat detection and insemination were not done at the right time. This may reflect a certain slakness in the way the paid and trained secretary; village's extension officers and field officers have fulfilled their responsibility in this regard. Thus the animals' husbandry programme has not been performed well.

Table 4. 4.5: Breeding Rate

S.No	Year TDCS	1996-97	1997-98	1998-99	Rate of change in percentage
Bastar					
1.	Tukaja wali	0.1974	0.0865	0.0356	-81.97
2.	Korenar	0.1890	0.538	0.0217	-88.52
3.	Konargaon	0.2019	0.0612	0.0512	-74.20
4.	Chogenmulla	0.1920	0.0819	0.0881	-54.11
5.	Karamar	0.2218	0.1026	0.0221	-90.03
	Average	0.20042	0.0772	0.04374	

(Contd.)

(Contd. Table 4.4.5)

S.No	Year TDCS	1996-97	1997-98	1998-99	Rate of change in percentage
Mandla					
6.	Babli	0.1628	0.0886	0.0120	-92.63
7.	Khari	0.1690	0.0920	0.0690	-59.17
8.	Khandehi	0.1750	0.0960	0.1021	-41.66
9.	Bhilai	0.1630	0.1040	0.0996	-38.90
10.	Bhapsa	0.1596	0.0897	0.0901	-43.55
	Average	0.16588	0.09412	0.07456	

(Contd.)

(Contd.Table 4.4.5)

S.No	*Year TDCS*	*1996-97*	*1997-98*	*1998-99*	*Rate of change in percentage*
Surguja					
11.	Pampapur	0.1468	0.0769	0.0870	-40.74
12.	Sonpur	0.1506	0.1102	0.1036	-31.21
13.	Kailashpur	0.1519	0.0926	0.0989	-34.89
14.	Silfili	0.2018	0.1306	0.1076	-23.32
15.	Madluvan	0.2601	0.0912	0.0760	-91.59
	Average	0.2346	0.1003	0.09462	

(Contd.)

(Contd. Table 4.4.5)

S.No	Year TDCS	1996-97	1997-98	1998-99	Rate of change in percentage
Raigarh					
16.	Basanpali	0.2242	0.1019	0.1001	-55.35
17.	Pata	0.2196	0.1604	0.1196	-45.54
18.	Jamura	0.2066	0.1517	0.1246	-39.97
19.	Raniguda	0.2255	0.01022	0.1096	-45.69
20.	Barpali	0.1967	0.1170	0.1206	-38.69
	Average	0.21452	0.12664	0.1149	-33.51

(Contd.)

(Contd. Table 4.4.5)

S.No	*Year TDCS*	*1996-97*	*1997-98*	*1998-99*	*Rate of change in percentage*
Jhabua					
21.	Gopalpur	0.3280	0.2250	0.2181	-33.89
22.	Tarkhedi	0.3172	0.2180	0.2097	-40.72
23.	Chhayan	0.3094	0.1924	0.1834	-26.09
24.	Jhadki	0.3296	0.2026	0.2436	-57.98
25.	Jharadabarr	0.3104	0.02868	0.2924	
	Average	0.31892	0.22496	0.21576	

Pregnancy Rate

This measures the ratio of the number of detected pregnant cattle to the number of cattle. This indicator also helps to evaluate the efficiency of secretaries and VEOs in detecting pregnancies the data on pregnancy rate for the three years 1996-97, 97-98 and 98-99 and the rate of change are presented in Table 4.4.6

A thorough look at the table reveals that the pregnancy rates ranged form as low as 21/1000 to as high as 160/1000. In the year 1996-97, the pregnancy rate in all the 25 TDCS was move than 100/1000. But in the succeeding years, the pregnancy rates come down drastically. Hence the rate of change in all the twenty-five TDCS was recorded as negative. This shows that the animal husbandry activities under the ITDDP in these tribal villages were not performed well.

Thus the two indicators breeding rate and pregnancy rate was found to reduce over the three-year period thereby causing the failure of the animal husbandry programme activities of ITDDP. The success of the program in increasing the number of productive animals over the three years period was actually responsible for the success of the tribal dairy cooperative societies in these tribal districts. On the other hand, productive animals got reduced due to decreasing breeding and pregnancy rates and dry animals had increased in number adversely affecting the dairy enterprise here.

Table 4. 4.6: Pregnancy Rate

S.No	*Year TDCS*	*1996-97*	*1997-98*	*1998-99*	*Rate of change in percentage*
	Bastar				
1.	Tukaja wali	0.1384	0.0841	0.0210	-84.82
2.	Korenar	0.1164	0.0676	0.0438	-62.37
3.	Konargaon	0.1089	0.0768	0.0575	-47.20
4.	Chogenmulla	0.1249	0.0640	0.0378	-69.74
5.	Karamar	0.1420	0.0819	0.0372	-73.80
	Average	0.12612	0.07488	0.03946	

(Contd.)

(Contd. Table 4.4.6)

S.No	*Year TDCS*	*1996-97*	*1997-98*	*1998-99*	*Rate of change in percentage*
Mandla					
6.	Babli	0.0978	0.0415	0.0320	-67.28
7.	Khari	0.1027	0.0687	0.0396	-63.33
8.	Khandehi	0.1080	0.0542	0.0216	-66.98
9.	Bhilai	0.0972	0.0460	0.0321	-54.24
10.	Bhapsa	0.0896	0.0655	0.0410	-61.15
	Average	0.09906	0.05518	0.03326	

(Contd.)

(Contd. Table 4.4.6)

S.No	Year TDCS	1996-97	1997-98	1998-99	Rate of change in percentage
Surguja					
11.	Pampapur	0.0978	0.0743	0.0380	-61.16
12.	Sonpur	0.1098	0.0514	0.0212	-80.69
13.	Kailashpur	0.1125	0.0676	0.0484	-56.70
14.	Silfili	0.1180	0.0510	0.0378	-67.97
15.	Madluvan	0.1240	0.0721	0.0628	-49.35
	Average	0.11242	0.06338	0.04164	

(Contd.)

(Contd. Table 4.4.6)

S.No	*Year TDCS*	*1996-97*	*1997-98*	*1998-99*	*Rate of change in percentage*
Raigarh					
16.	Basanpali	0.1314	0.0809	0.0381	-71.00
17.	Pata	0.1296	0.0978	0.0475	-63.46
18.	Jamura	0.1155	0.0694	0.0334	-70.99
19.	Raniguda	0.1244	0.0826	0.0632	-49.99
20.	Barpali	0.1396	0.0920	0.0712	-48.99
	Average	0.1281	0.08254	0.05068	

(Contd.)

(Contd. Table 4.4.6)

S.No	Year TDCS	1996-97	1997-98	1998-99	Rate of change in percentage
Jhabua					
21.	Gopalpur	0.1421	0.0810	0.0720	-49.33
22.	Tarkhedi	0.1396	0.0900	0.0810	-14.98
23.	Chhayan	0.1507	0.1020	0.0758	-49.70
24.	Jhadki	0.1318	0.0921	0.0671	-49.08
25.	Jharadabarr	0.1604	0.1124	0.0962	-40.03
	Average	0.14492	0.0955	0.07842	

(c) Breeding Behaviour

This et of target indicators deal with the age at first calving ad inter-calving period which help evaluating the breeding behaviour of cattle here.

Low productivity of milch animals in India has been attributed to ate age at first calving, long calving intervals, short lactation period, low average daily milk yield and low average body weight at birth (Acharya and Huria, 1980). Only to factors were studied here-age at first calving (in months) and inter-calving period (in months).

Age at First Calving

This indicator was measured as the age of the cow at her first calving, and measured in months. The services provided by the trained secretary VEOs and supervision had been directed to lower the age at first calving among the milch cattle under each TDCS.

A cursory look at the table 4.4.7 reveals that in all the TDCSs the age at first calving was higher than the national average (50 months) computed in 1980 (Shah, Tripathi and Desai, 1980). In the villages of Mandla and Surguja, it ranged from 62 to 63 months, in villages of Bastar and Raigarh it was around 61 months. But in the villages of Jhabua it was around 55 months on an average. It was also found showing negative rate of change in many TDCSs indicating an improvement of the animal health and nutrition in these tribal villages.

Table 4. 4.7: Age at first calving in months

S.No	*Year TDCS*	*1996-97*	*1997-98*	*1998-99*	*Rate of change in percentage*
Bastar					
1.	Tukajawali	62.10	62.00	62.00	-0.16
2.	Korenar	61.80	61.00	62.10	-0.49
3.	Konargaon	60.98	60.50	60.00	-1.61
4.	Chogenmulla	61.05	61.00	61.00	-0.08
5.	Karamar	61.90	61.50	61.80	-0.16
	Average	1.56	61.20	61.38	

(Contd.)

(Contd. Table 4.4.7)

S.No	Year TDCS	1996-97	1997-98	1998-99	Rate of change in percentage
Mandla					
6.	Babli	63.40	63.50	63.50	-0.86
7.	Khari	62.80	62.50	63.10	-0.00
8.	Khandehi	61.75	62.10	62.75	-0.07
9.	Bhilai	63.00	62.80	62.25	-0.24
10.	Bhapsa	62.10	62.00	61.40	-0.32
	Average	62.61	62.58	62.60	

(Contd.)

(Contd. Table 4.4.7)

S.No	Year TDCS	1996-97	1997-98	1998-99	Rate of change in percentage
Surguja					
11.	Pampapur	6.05	63.00	63.50	-0.86
12.	Sonpur	63.10	63.00	63.10	-0.00
13.	Kailashpur	62.80	62.00	62.75	-0.07
14.	Silfili	62.40	62.20	62.25	-0.24
15.	Madluvan	61.20	61.10	61.40	-0.32
	Average	62.71	62.26	62.60	

(Contd.)

(Contd. Table 4.4.7)

S.No	Year TDCS	1996-97	1997-98	1998-99	Rate of change in percentage
Raigarh					
16.	Basanpali	61.20	61.10	61.30	-0.16
17.	Pata	61.50	61.20	61.80	0.48
18.	Jamura	61.00	61.00	61.20	0.16
19.	Raniguda	61.10	61.00	61.50	0.65
20.	Barpali	61.30	64.05	61.25	-0.08
	Average	61.22	61.67	61.41	

(Contd.)

(Contd.Table 4.4.7)

S.No	*Year TDCS*	*1996-97*	*1997-98*	*1998-99*	*Rate of change in percentage*
Jhabua					
21.	Gopalpur	54.40	54.10	56.00	2.94
22.	Tarkhedi	52.80	52.70	52.00	-1.50
23.	Chhayan	57.18	57.10	55.00	-3.81
24.	Jhadki	58.50	58.35	58.00	-0.85
25.	Jharadabar	55.10	55.00	55.00	-0.18

Inter-calving Period

This indicator was measured as the number of months taken between two successive calvings. The inter-calving period need to be shortened for the success of these dairy enterprise and the services provided by the VEOs and supervisors were directed to that effect. The data on these indicators were presented in Table 4.4.8.

A thorough look at the data in the table reveals that the average inter-calving period in the twenty five TDCS ranged from 21 to 24 months which was quite greater than the national average (20 months) computed in 1980 (Shah, Tripathi and Desai, 1980). It was found that the situation, as regards this indicator, was worse in Mandla and Surguja districts than in Bastar and Raigarh districts. Only in Jhabua district the inter-calving period was close to the nation found to be seen in Jhabua district, through rate of fall was marginal.

On both these target indicators dealing with breeding behaviour, the performance of the animal husbandry activities under ITDDP was found to be not successfully in building up the health of the cattle and also on the breeding behaviour of the herd.

(D) Nutritional Standard of the Herd

The quality and quantity of feed available exercise a powerful influence on the milk yields per animals as well as the breeding behaviour of the herd. Under this group, three target indicators were considered: (i) sale of concentrate cattle feed

Table 4. 4.8: Inter-calving Period in Months

S.No	Year TDCS	1996-97	1997-98	1998-99	Rate of change in percentage
Bastar					
1.	Tukajawali	22.50	21.50	22.00	-2.22
2.	Korenar	23.10	23.50	23.60	2.16
3.	Konargaon	21.80	22.70	23.00	5.50
4.	Chogenmulla	22.50	22.25	22.75	1.11
5.	Karamar	21.40	21.25	22.80	6.54
	Average	22.26	22.24	22.83	

(Contd.)

(Contd. Table 4.4.8)

S.No	*Year TDCS*	*1996-97*	*1997-98*	*1998-99*	*Rate of change in percentage*
Mandla					
6.	Babli	24.00	24.00	24.00	0.0
7.	Khari	24.10	24.25	24.20	0.41
8.	Khandehi	24.25	24.40	24.50	1.03
9.	Bhilai	24.80	24.40	24.45	-1.41
10.	Bhapsa	24.30	24.50	24.55	1.03
	Average	24.29	24.31	24.34	

(Contd.)

(Contd. Table 4.4.8)

S.No	Year TDCS	1996-97	1997-98	1998-99	Rate of change in percentage
Surguja					
11.	Pampapur	23.80	23.40	23.45	-1.47
12.	Sonpur	23.10	23.20	23.10	0.0
13.	Kailashpur	23.80	23.75	23.60	-0.84
14.	Silfili	23.25	23.40	23.25	0.0
15.	Madluvan	22.95	22.50	23.20	1.09
	Average	23.38	23.45	23.32	

(Contd.)

(Contd. Table 4.4.8)

S.No	*Year TDCS*	*1996-97*	*1997-98*	*1998-99*	*Rate of change in percentage*
Raigarh					
16.	Basanpali	22.10	22.20	22.50	1.80
17.	Pata	22.20	22.00	22.10	-0.45
18.	Jamura	22.50	22.40	22.25	-1.11
19.	Raniguda	23.10	23.00	23.10	0.0
20.	Barpali	23.50	23.20	23.25	-1.06
	Average	22.68	22.86	22.64	

(Contd.)

(Contd. Table 4.4.8)

S.No	*Year TDCS*	*1996-97*	*1997-98*	*1998-99*	*Rate of change in percentage*
Jhabua					
21.	Gopalpur	21.50	22.00	22.00	2.33
22.	Tarkhedi	21.50	21.00	21.20	-1.40
23.	Chhayan	22.75	21.80	21.50	-1.09
24.	Jhadki	21.50	21.20	21.10	-1.86
25.	Jharadabar	21.80	21.00	21.00	-3.67
	Average	21.81	21.4	21.36	

(Rs. per year) per milch animals (ii) supply of fodder seed (Rs. per year) per milch animals and (iii) grazing land (acres) available per milch animals. These three indicators cover three aspects of animal nutrition-available grazing land, available concentrate cattle feed and available fodder seed so that tribal farmers how these seeds and raise green fodder crops and feed their cattle.

Sale of Concentrate Cattle Feed

Under the ITDDP, a group of activities were undertaken in each TDCS that aim to improve the nutritional standard of the herd. The concentrate cattle feed was made available under each TDCS on sale to tribal farmers. This was supplied to all the twenty-five TDCS only upto 1996-97. So the data as available was presented in Table 4.4.9.

As can be seen from the table, the sale of concentrate cattle feed in rupees per year per milch animals ranged form Rs. 22 to Rs. 54, which can be considered as much lower than desired. Only in two districts, the situation was a little better as it averaged around Rs. 45 milch animals per year.

Supply of fodder seed (Rs. per year) per milch animals

Under the ITDDP, a fodder development officer in each district whom taken care of fodder crops being raised and fed to cattle by the tribal farmers. The fodder seeds-usually fodder fowar

Table 4. 4.9: Sale of Concentrates Cattle Feed and Supply of Fodder Seed per Milch Animal (value Rs. /year) in 1996-97

S.No	*Year TDCS*	*Sale of concentrate cattle Per milch animal*	*Supply of fodder seed per milch animal*
Bastar			
1.	Tukajawali	22.60	11.54
2.	Korenar	22.01	08.20
3.	Konargaon	22.16	09.36
4.	Chogenmulla	21.98	10.50
5.	Karamar	22.69	09.25
	Average	22.30	09.77

(Contd.)

(Contd.Table 4.4.9)

S.No	*Year TDCS*	*Sale of concentrate cattle Per milch animal*	*Supply of fodder seed per milch animal*
Mandla			
6.	Babli	21.75	07.50
7.	Khari	22.95	08.75
8.	Khandehi	22.10	07.75
9.	Bhilai	22.86	08.00
10.	Bhapsa	22.01	08.25
	Average	22.13	07.95

(Contd.)

(Contd. Table 4.4.9)

S.No	*Year TDCS*	*Sale of concentrate cattle Per milch animal*	*Supply of fodder seed per milch animal*
Surguja			
11.	Pampapur	23.10	12.96
12.	Sonpur	22.97	12.50
13.	Kailashpur	23.10	10.00
14.	Silfili	23.21	09.00
15.	Madluvan	33.60	08.00
	Average	27.20	10.49

(Contd.)

(Contd. Table 4.4.9)

S.No	Year TDCS	Sale of concentrate cattle Per milch animal	Supply of fodder seed per milch animal
Raigarh			
16.	Basanpali	44.16	10.50
17.	Pata	43.60	15.75
18.	Jamura	48.10	14.50
19.	Raniguda	42.96	12.50
20.	Barpali	53.96	12.50
	Average	46.56	13.15

(Contd.)

(Contd. Table 4.4.9)

S.No	Year TDCS	Sale of concentrate cattle Per milch animal	Supply of fodder seed per milch animal
Jhabua			
21.	Gopalpur	44.18	15.50
22.	Tarkhedi	53.68	16.00
23.	Chhayan	34.06	15.00
24.	Jhadki	53.12	14.00
25.	Jharadabar	44.86	18.00
	Average	45.98	15.70

and berseem were given to tribal farmers and their cropping was monitored. This was also stopped after 1996-97. The data as available for one year are presented in Table 4.4.9.

As can be seen from the table, the fodder seeds supplied per milch animal per year ranged from Rs. 8.25 to Rs. 18.00. The situation was far from satisfactory in the districts of Mandla, Bastar and Surguja but a little better in Raigarh and Jhabua districts.

Grazing Land per Milch Animals per Year

The usual practice of tribal farmers in these villages was to allow the cattle to go out for grazing in the nearby pasturelands of the village and nearby forest. The traditional way of grazing livestock follows a cyclical pattern that depends on the specific characteristics of the village concerned (Damodaran, 1987). During the post-harvest season, cattle usually feed on the crop stubble, later in the year, tank beds and forestland are used and during the monsoon the available pastureland in the village, the waste lands and forests are used. The data on the indicators was computed using the formula mentioned already in the chapter on research methodology. The data were available for three years and hence rate of change was also calculated. The data are presented in Table 4.4.10. An can be seen from the table, the available grazing land per milch animal was found to decline in all the twenty five TDCSs over the three year period.

Table 4. 4.10: Grazing Land per Adult

S.No	*Year TDCS*	*1996-97*	*1997-98*	*1998-99*	*Rate of change in percentage*
Bastar					
1.	Tukajawali	0.940	0.843	0.822	-12.54
2.	Korenar	0.822	0.801	0.763	-7.11
3.	Konargaon	0.921	0.812	0.754	-18.14
4.	Chogenmulla	0.787	0.603	0.555	-29.58
5.	Karamar	0.882	0.744	0.644	26.96
	Average	0.870	0.760	0.708	

(Contd.)

(Contd. Table 4.4.10)

S.No	Year TDCS	1996-97	1997-98	1998-99	Rate of change in percentage
Mandla					
6.	Babli	0.781	0.695	0.595	-23.88
7.	Khari	0.656	0.628	0.587	-10.43
8.	Khandehi	0.597	0.523	0.514	-13.83
9.	Bhilai	0.657	0.557	0.513	-20.97
10.	Bhapsa	0.785	0.674	0.592	-24.59
	Average	0.695	0.616	0.562	

(Contd.)

(Contd. Table 4.4.10)

S.No	*Year TDCS*	*1996-97*	*1997-98*	*1998-99*	*Rate of change in percentage*
Surguja					
11.	Pampapur	0.964	0.987	0.790	-18.09
12.	Sonpur	0.845	0.736	0.672	-20.47
13.	Kailashpur	0.766	0.660	0.650	-15.19
14.	Silfili	0.835	0.732	0.702	-15.89
15.	Madluvan	0.955	0.887	0.763	-20.15
	Average	0.874	0.821	0.715	

(Contd.)

(Contd. Table 4.4.10)

S.No	*Year TDCS*	*1996-97*	*1997-98*	*1998-99*	*Rate of change in percentage*
Raigarh					
16.	Basanpali	0.864	0.774	0.755	-12.63
17.	Pata	0.926	0.862	0.872	-5.84
18.	Jamura	0.987	0.880	0.864	-0.11
19.	Raniguda	0.995	0.844	0.810	-18.70
20.	Barpali	0.887	0.745	0.724	-16.47
	Average	0.932	0.821	0.805	

(Contd.)

(Contd. Table 4.4.10)

S.No	*Year TDCS*	*1996-97*	*1997-98*	*1998-99*	*Rate of change in percentage*
Jhabua					
21.	Gopalpur	0.764	0.664	0.625	-10.38
22.	Tarkhedi	0.832	0.763	0.735	-12.88
23.	Chhayan	0.742	0.629	0.608	-18.81
24.	Jhadki	0.892	0.763	0.722	-10.99
25.	Jharadabar	0.972	0.850	0.814	-16.60
	Average	0.841	0.734	0.700	

It ranged from 0.514 acres per milch animal to 0.995 acres per milch animal. The situation got worsened in Mandla Bastar and Surguja. In Jhabua and Raigarh, the situation was a little better as compared to other districts. The grazing land per milch animal got reduced but in these two districts the use of concentrate feed and fodder crop rising were better and the overall nutritional standards in these to districts had improved.

Among all the four groups of achievement target indicators, the first group of indicators was studied to understand the long-term build up of the herd. The vaccination of cattle was seen as a very important practice to be invariably adopted in all the TDCS for all the milch animals, and especially the female calves, the future milch producers of the herd. Vaccination rate was directly linked to the herd mortality and female calf mortality.

Similarly the breeding practices and breeding behaviour of the herd are quite related indicators. The breeding rate and pregnancy rate need to be monitored regularly by the VEOs, supervision and veterinary doctor as they directly affect the build up of the herd.

The breeding behaviour age at first calving and inter-calving period were also related to the nutritional standard indicators. Breeding behaviour was found to be directly effected by the health and nutrition of the young female calves.

All these indicators increase were found to be e directly impacting the dairy development in these tribal villages. The efforts of staff under the ITDDP were found to be quite lacking and not resulting in positive impact on dairy development in these tribal villages.

Economic Performance Indicators

Till now, the achievement target indicators have been discussed. Now an attempt has been made to look at the economic performance of the tribal dairy cooperative societies. The impact of ITDDP can be seen on a few indicators, which have measured. These are 1) membership strength, number of milk sellers in both lean and flush seasons, the milk procurement (in litres) by each TDCS and the met profit made by each TDCS. The data were available for all the three years from 1996-97 to 1998-99. The rate of change was also calculated for understanding the trends.

Members and Milk Sellers in TDCS

Under the ITDDP, organising tribal dairy farmers into tribal dairy cooperative societies was the main activity under which all the other animal husbandry improvement activities were undertaken. A tribal dairy farmer needs to become a member by paying Rs. 11 to enjoy the benefits of the programme. Among the members, only a few sell their surplus milk to the TDCS. In the flush season, when milk supply is move, move milk supplier sell milk and in the dry or lean

Table 4. 4.11: Total members of TDCS and Total Milk Suppliers in Lean and Flush Season

TDCS	*1996-97*			*1997-98*			*1998-99*		
	TM	*MSLS*	*MSFS*	*TM*	*MSLS*	*MSFS*	*TM*	*MSLS*	*MSFS*
Bastar									
1. Tukajawali	110	58	75	112	50	70	100	40	60
2. Korenar	98	56	65	108	50	58	102	38	49
3. Konargaon	88	45	62	101	40	55	95	35	50
4. Chogenmull	102	50	65	102	48	58	96	40	51
5. Karamar	99	51	67	105	46	61	97	37	53
Average	99	51	67	105	46	61	97	37	53
Mondla									
6. Babli	98	55	70	100	51	61	80	40	58
7. Khari	92	46	62	92	45	56	90	42	50
8. Khandehi	82	45	58	85	40	52	81	38	48
9. Bhilai	76	40	55	80	38	50	77	35	42
10. Bhapsa	110	39	68	100	30	55	94	30	45
Average	91	45	62	91	40	54	84	37	48

(Contd.)

(Contd. Table 4.4.11)

TDCS	1996-97			1997-98			1998-99		
	TM	MSLS	MSFS	TM	MSLS	MSFS	TM	MSLS	MSFS
Surguja									
11 Pampapur	80	40	45	85	38	40	80	30	35
12 Sonpur	89	45	58	98	40	55	82	35	50
13 Kailashpur	109	42	60	110	36	60	95	30	52
14. Selfili	56	40	51	60	35	50	50	32	48
15. S.madhuvan	50	40	50	50	36	40	43	28	32
Average	76	41	52	80	37	49	70	31	43
Raigarh									
16 Basanpali	120	45	60	125	40	62	100	38	55
17 Pata	108	58	70	108	50	65	98	42	58
18 Jamura	105	48	52	110	40	48	100	28	40
19 Raniguda	112	50	65	115	50	60	105	45	55
20 Basanpali	135	60	78	140	55	65	120	51	58
Average	116	52	65	119	47	60	105	45	55
Jhabua									
21 Gopalpur	107	60	70	116	55	75	120	58	80
22 Tarkhedi	125	55	78	128	60	82	130	62	86
23 Chhayan	89	60	75	100	60	82	125	65	91
24 Jhadki	95	55	70	115	60	75	120	65	89
25 Jharadabar	110	70	95	125	75	100	135	80	115
Average	105	60	77	116	62	82	126	66	84

season, less number of tribal people supply milk to the milk collection centers of TDCS. The data are presented in table Table 4.4.11.

As can be seen from the table, the total members and consequently total milk suppliers in both seasons got reduced very drastically in Surguja, Mandla and Bastar. In Raigarh the membership got stabilized at around 100 but in Jhabua, the members and milk sellers actually increased over the years. The milk suppliers in lean season were about 50 per cent and in flush season were about nearly 70 per cent on an average. This can be seen as indicators of the positive impact of ITDDP on the tribal dairy development of Jhabua district.

Milk Procurement

As has been already mentioned in the section I of this chapter, the integrated tribal dairy development programme envisages organizing assured and regular milk procurement through its milk collection centres from tribal dairy farmers. This indicator directly measures the total number of litres of milk procured by each tribal dairy cooperative society in a year. The milk thus procured will be transported in milk cows in a truck to the District Dairy Cooperatives Union Dairy where it is sold, chilled, pasteurized and stored and further distributed and sold to urban consumers. Milk procured in litres in three years by each TDCS was presented in Table 4.4.12.

Table 4. 4.12: Milk Procurement (lits) by TDCS

S.No	*Year TDCS*	*1996-97*	*1997-98*	*1998-99*	*Rate of change in percentage*
Bastar					
1.	Tukajawali	53200	48000	41500.0	-21.99
2.	Korenar	56800	53250	46128.0	-18.79
3.	Konargaon	46700	39000	34000.0	-27.19
4.	Chogenmulla	49850	42400	36480.0	-26.82
5.	Karamar	52115	47100	42810.0	-17.85
	Average	51733	46350	40184	

(Contd.)

(Contd. Table 4.4.12)

S.No	Year TDCS	1996-97	1997-98	1998-99	Rate of change in percentage
Mandla					
6.	Babli	50950	45120	39200	-23.06
7.	Khari	48128	40400	36800	-23.54
8.	Khandehi	43110	38100	30400	-29.54
9.	Bhilai	38050	34115	31123	-18.20
10.	Bhapsa	42800	37550	33450	-21.85
	Average	44608	39057	34195	

(Contd.)

(Contd. Table 4.4.12)

S.No	Year TDCS	1996-97	1997-98	1998-99	Rate of change in percentage
Surguja					
11.	Pampapur	32680	31200	28260	-13.53
12.	Sonpur	41200	38000	34350	-16.26
13.	Kailashpur	45620	45620.5	39800	-26.57
14.	Silfili	46800	39950	32620	-30.30
15.	Madluvan	38050	36125	30058	-21.00
	Average	40870	37015	31758	

(Contd.)

(Contd. Table 4.4.12)

S.No	*Year TDCS*	*1996-97*	*1997-98*	*1998-99*	*Rate of change in percentage*
Raigarh					
16.	Basanpali	52500	51000	44180	-15.85
17.	Pata	64185	57500	50800	-20.85
18.	Jamura	55280	44800	38050	-31.17
19.	Raniguda	57500	55000	47580	-17.25
20.	Basanpali	69010	63500	54510	-21.01
	Average	59695	54360	47024	

(Contd.)

(Contd. Table 4.4.12)

S.No	Year TDCS	1996-97	1997-98	1998-99	Rate of change in percentage
Jhabua					
21.	Gopalpur	78153	75000	82800	5.95
22.	Tarkhedi	79898	85210	88100	10.27
23.	Chhayan	81835	86350	93810	14.63
24.	Jhadki	75620	81105	92400	22.19
25.	Jharadabar	99650	105000	117800	18.21
	Average	83031	86533	94982	

A cursory look at the table reveals that there was a fall in the rate of milk procurement in the four district-Bastar, Mandla, Surguja and Raigarh to about 20 per cent. Only in Jhabua district, there was an increase in milk procurement to about 15 per cent. As regards, the total milk procured by each TDCs, it was around 40 thousand litres per TDCS per year in the four districts. But in Jhabua, the total milk procured was also more and was around 90 thousand litres per TDCS per year. There was a very high degree of positive impact of ITDDP on milk procurement only on the five TDCSs studied in Jhabua district. But in the other TDCSs in four districts, the impact was positive to begin with but withered aay in the succeeding years. But the decline was marginal as the initial quantity of milk procured was also at lower levels.

Net Profit of TDCS

A trained and paid secretary who is usually an educated unemployed tribal youth looked after each Tribal Dairy Cooperative Society. This secretary is usually assisted by two assistants who helps him collecting milk samples for testing, for measuring the milk supplied by each member milk supplier, milk fat testing, carrying milk cows to the main road where milk collection trucks pass by and other sundry jobs. This staffs are paid by the TDCSs. In addition, the expenditure includes milk testing equipment (including test tubes and chemicals), records and registers, etc. Cattle feed is also bought by TDCS from the District Union and sold to members. All these expenditure has to be convered by the TDCS, from the milk produced and solf to the Union Dairy. The net profit made by each TDCS indicators the financial health of the TDCS. If a particular TDCS was able to meet the expenses, pay the members the amount of money due for the milk procured and still able to a manage a net profit, it usually also pays a amount of bonus to its members. It addition animals health improvement activities will also be taken up. The data related to net profits made by TDCSs and rate of change over years are presented in Table 4.4.13.

A cursory look at the data in the table reveals that the profits made by the TDCSs in the four districts declined very drastically over the three-year period. The fall in the net profit was greatest upto 90 per cent in a few TDCSs best was around 50 per cent on an average. In Mandla and Surguja, the situation was worse than in Bastar and Raigarh. But in Jhabua, the situation was much better with an increase in net profits over the years at about 11 per cent on an average and a total average net profit of about Rs. 26000 per year per TDCS.

Thus the economic performance indicators have shown a decreasing trend in Bastar, Mandla, Surguja and Raigarh, but an increasing trend in Jhabua. A ray of hope was seen on the horizons of the tribal villages of Jhabua where the

Table 4. 4.13: Net Profit of TDCS

S.No	*Year TDCS*	*1996-97*	*1997-98*	*1998-99*	*Rate of change in percentage*
Bastar					
1.	Tukajawali	10788	5962	4932	-54.28
2.	Korenar	11678	9447	7820	-33.04
3.	Konargaon	11196	8562	4380	-60.88
4.	Chogenmulla	13436	9327	6461	-51.91
5.	Karamar	15851	10482	9035	-43.00
	Average	12590	8756	6526	

(Contd.)

(Contd. Table 4.4.13)

S.No	Year TDCS	1996-97	1997-98	1998-99	Rate of change in percentage
Mandla					
6.	Babli	10250	6856	3848	-33.11
7.	Khari	9652	3418	1081	-88.80
8.	Khandehi	8785	2667	1002	-88.59
9.	Bhilai	11425	5750	2819	-75.33
10.	Bhapsa	12835	7428	4812	-62.51
	Average	105890	5224	3676	

(Contd.)

(Contd. Table 4.4.13)

S.No	*Year TDCS*	*1996-97*	*1997-98*	*1998-99*	*Rate of change in percentage*
Surguja					
11.	Pampapur	6130	5488	4532	-26.07
12.	Sonpur	8281	2875	2318	-72.01
13.	Kailashpur	10378	6655	2180	-78.99
14.	Silfili	10280	7833	3005	-70.77
15.	Madhuvan				
	Average	8836	5200	2631	

(Contd.)

(Contd. Table 4.4.13)

S.No	*Year TDCS*	*1996-97*	*1997-98*	*1998-99*	*Rate of change in percentage*
Raigarh					
16.	Basanpali	12395	10250	8375	-32.43
17.	Pata	15251	11850	7310	-52.07
18.	Jamura	10388	9335	4388	-57.76
19.	Raniguda	12850	10688	6816	-46.96
20.	Basanpali	13210	9624	5482	-58.99
	Average	12819	10353	6474	

(Contd.)

(Contd. Table 4.4.13)

S.No	*Year TDCS*	*1996-97*	*1997-98*	*1998-99*	*Rate of change in percentage*
Jhabua					
21.	Gopalpur	20651	21225	22810	10.45
22.	Tarkhedi	22365	23110	24635	10.15
23.	Chhayan	23165	24650	24850	6.41
24.	Jhadki	18950	20333	23165	22.24
25.	Jharadabar	25650	.26815	26950	5.09
	Average	22156	23227	26182	

improvement in the dairy development and the possible positive impact on the lives of tribal people were seen.

A Sysmptic Note

Among the various achievement target indicators, the most crucial were herd mortality female calf mortality rate, vaccination rate, breeding rate, pregnancy rate, age at first calving and inter-calving period. These indicators have clearly brought out the possible impact of ITDDP on the dairy development in the tribal villages and districts. The results had clearly slow that the impact of ITDDP on the various indicators of dairy development in these tribal areas was far from satisfactory except only in Jhabua. The case of Jhabua was a study in contrast as clear positive impact was seen in all the achievement target indicators.

On the economic performance, the same story continued with declining economic performance in Bastar, Mandla, Surguja and Raigarh. Jhabua had presented in a ray of hope in the darkness as the tribal dairy cooperative societies prospered very well. Some of the policies followed by these TDCS in this district were worth appreciation. Only in these TDCSs, the member's participation and involvement in dairy development was very good and all the members had received regularly bonus along with all the veterinary services including timely vaccination, veterinary treatment, heat detection, timely insemination, proper animal nutrition and health care.

Thus the positive impact had also brought about a new cycle of progress among the tribal dairy farmers of this district.

Section V: Opinion of Respondents and TDCS Officials on the ITDDP Activities

Tribal farmers and the office bearers of tribal dariy cooperative society run the integrated tribal dariy development programme activities in their villages. The government of Madhya Pradesh had established suitable infrastructure at state, district and village level to run this programme for the welfare of the tribal people. Hence the participation of tribal people in this dairy development programme is curcial to the success of the programme. In this connection, an attempt has been made to know the opinion of the tribal farmers on the relevance, usefulness of the activities undertaken in the Integrated Tribal Dairy Development Programme.

A mention on this variable has already been made in the section II where the summated scores of opinion were categoriezed into three groups less favourable, moderately favourable and highly favourable. It has also been found that the beneficiary tribal farmer respondents had a modertely favourable opinion on the ITDDP programme. Here in this section, an attempt has been made to context anlayse the statements of opnion. Here the opinion of TDCS officials was also studied. The results were presented in Table 4.5.1.

Table 4. 5.1: Opinion of the Respondents Towards Integrated Tribal Dairy Development Programme (ITDDP)

S.No	*Statement*	*Percentage of respondents agreeing with statement*		
		Beneficiaries (N=100)	*Non-Beneficiaries (N=100)*	*TDCS Officials (N=25)*
A				
1	Improvement in agricultural knowledge after this programme	55	15	48
2	Acquired skills in animal husbandry & dairy management	65	35	84
3	Acquired skills in fodder production	64	40	92
4	Facilities for animal health care increased	80	70	88

(Contd.)

(Contd. Table 4.5.1)

S.No	Statement	Percentage of respondents agreeing with statement		
		Beneficiaries (N=100)	Non-Beneficiaries (N=100)	TDCS Officials (N=25)
5	Stall feeding of animals	60	15	40
6	Benefits of the dairy development programme made available	90	30	40
7	Marketing facilities increased	88	38	56
8	Employment opportunities increased	85	48	72
9	ITDDP is doing satistically work	60	20	80

(Contd.)

(Contd. Table 4.5.1)

S.No	Statement	Percentage of respondents agreeing with statement		
		Beneficiaries (N=100)	Non-Beneficiaries (N=100)	TDCS Officials (N=25)
B				
10	Family income has increased due to move milk production	70	55	100
11	Standard of living improved	75	60	96
12	Introduced change in life style	56	62	76
13	Improvement in food habits and food availability	51	43	64
14	Increase in milk consumption	55	15	45
15	Change in credit behaviour	52	46	52

(Contd.)

(Contd. Table 4.5.1)

S.No	*Statement*	*Percentage of respondents agreeing with statement*		
		Beneficiaries (N=100)	*Non-Beneficiaries (N=100)*	*TDCS Officials (N=25)*
C				
16	Social participaticn increased	65	35	70
17	Introduced changes in tribal leadership pattern	68	53	60
18	Improved social respect in tribal community after accepting this ITDD programme	63	50	60

As presented in the table, the statements can be seen under three major groups one set of statements deal with the programmes and its immediate effects on improvement in knowledge and skill of tribal farmers (1-9), second set of statement deal with the immediate short term consequences on the life style and living standards (10-15) and the third set of statements deal with the long-term benefits or consequences on tribal life.

A. Improvement in Knowledge, Skill and Adoption of Improved Dariy Management Practices

A cursory look at the table reveals some interesting observations. Though there appears to be divided opinion on whether the ITDDP doing satisfactory work, there was unaninous agreement on such statements that with the introduction of ITDDP, many benefits had been accrued to the tribal people including increase in employment opportunity marketing facilities, animal health care facilities, benefits from TDCS, and also in the acquisition of skills and knolwedge of agricultural and dariy management practices including staff feeding, etc. Beneficiareis were found to perceive the benefits clearly than the non-beneficiaries.

B. Improvement in the Living Standards

Beneficiary tribal farmers respondents who became members of tribal dairy cooperative societies and enjoyed the benefits accruing from the society had developed a celarly favourable opinion abou the relevance and usefulness of the integrated tribal dairy development programme. The non-beneficiary respondetns had also seen the changes occuring in the villages due to the dairy cooperative society's work and developed a favourable opinion towards ITDDP. Family income had been opined to increase, with changes in life style, food habits, food availability, milk consumption, credit behaviour etc.

C. Consequence on Tribal Life

The Intergrated Tribal Diary Development Programme had brought about some changes in the tribal way of life. Some of the beneficiaries, non-beneficiaries and TDCS officials had opined that this programme had brought in a new social intitution in the tribal culture- the Tribal Dairy Co-operative Society that is a socio-economic organisation. For enjoying the benefits of the ITDDP, tribal farmers need to become members in the TDCS. This membership in TDCS had been perceived by many tribal people and 'respectable.

Thus this had been perccived as a source of social respect and social status. Thus many respondents had developed a positive opinion towards ITDDP that the participatoin in this programme brings with it not only economic benefits but also social benefits. Thus social particiaption had been found to increase thereby bringing about changes in leadership pattern in tribal lives. There may be possibility of evolution of new leaders coming from the new economic organisation the tribal dairy co-operative society which may have been seen as a threat to traditional leadership pattern in tribal societies.

From another point of view, the three groups of respondents have perceived these opinion statements differently. While it may be true and justified to say that the beneficiaries may agree with the opinion statements in large number because of their participation as members or vice versa, non-beneficiaries were also found to be not agreeing with the opinion statements in large members' bcasue of their non-participation. But the TDCS officials had a mixed agreement with many of the opinion statemtns. Some of the TDCS officials were paid government staff and some were honorary office bearers who were also tribal farmers and members of the society. They were the persons actually working for the ITDDP and might be findings that there still exist great gaps in providing benefits and increasing marketing facilities of members of the TDCS. At the outset, majority of the respondents had developed highly favourable opinion on some activties of ITDDP and moderately favourable opinion on some other activities of ITDDP.

Section VI: Socio-Economic Changes in Living Standards of Tribal after the Introduction of ITDDP

The integrated tribal dairy development programme had already been reported to be perceived as a relevant and useful programme for tribal people. In this section, an attempt has been made to study the changes that had occurred either directly or indirectly after the introduction of ITDDP in the respondent's villages. The direct changes were those changes in the socio-economic domain of tribals live that had occurred directly due to the implementation and acceptance of the ITDDP in the villages. The indirect changes were those changes that had occurred as a result of the above direct changes like changes in employment opportunities, concern for health, childrens' education, etc. The data indicating afirmative responses to the indicators of socio economic change are presented in Table 4.6.1.

The data presented in the Table 4.6.1 reveal that the beneficiary tribal farmer respondents had experienced some direct changes and some indirect changes in the socio-economic domain of their lives.

With the introduction of ITDDP in these villages, Tribal Dairy Cooperative Societies came into existence bringing an assured market for their milk. So dairy enterprise has been accepted by many (about 92 per cent) as a valuable alternative to alleviate their poverty. With TDCS, new inputs in terms of scientific dairy production technology, cattle feed and veterinary treatment has come to the villages. The villagers have accepted many of these technologies. As can be seen from the table, about 80 per cent of tribal farmers had started believing in government veterinary surgeons

Table 4. 6.1: Distribution of Beneficiary Respondents According to Socio-economic Changes (N=100)

S.No	*Areas and statements*	*Frequency*	*Ranks*
1.	Dairy as a profitable enterprise has been accepted	92	I
2.	Belief in Govt. Veternary surgeon treatment	80	IV
3.	Chaff cutter and stall feeding have become popular	88	III
4.	Raising fodder crops has increased	75	VI
5.	Construction of cattle shed become popular	68	XI
6.	Storage of fodder and forest grasses has increased	73	VIII
7.	Changes in knowledge in scientific dairy farming practice	59	XV
8.	Changes in knowledge in agricultural practices	76	V

(Contd.)

(Contd. Table 4.6.1)

S.No	Areas and statements	Frequency	Ranks
9a.	Employment opportunities have opened up	74	VII
9b.	Development orientation and participation in Govt. development programme has increased	53	VII
10.	Consumption of oil increased	75	VII
11.	Consumption of milk increased	69	X
12.	Consumption of vegetables increased	65	XII
13.	Consumption of sugar increased	62	XII
14.	Consumption of pulses increased	60	XIV
15.	Consumption of rice increased	56	XVII
16.	Consumption of wheat increased	42	XXII

(Contd.)

(Contd. Table 4.6.1)

S.No	*Areas and statements*	*Frequency*	*Ranks*
17.	Preventive measures against certain diseases has become popular	39	XXIII
18.	Expenditure on medical treatment of family members has increased	44	XXIV
19.	Consulting doctor at initial stage of illness for family members has become a regular practice	37	XXIV
20.	Started sending sons and daughters to school	65	XII
21.	Construction and renovation of houses	52	XIX
22.	Number of gold and silver ornaments have been purchased	49	XX
23.	Number of garmets in the family have increased	57	XVI
24.	Expenditure on marriage ceremony has increased	28	XXV

(Contd.)

(Contd. Table 4.6.1)

S.No	Areas and statements	Frequency	Ranks
25.	Urban contact has increased	69	X
26.	Life style has improved	58	XVI
27.	Consumption and material possession has increased	61	XIII
28.	Thrift habit and crientation for saving for future has increased	64	XIII
29.	Use of barter system reduced and use of money currency increased	91	II

treatment and about 88 per cent of the tribal dairy farmers had also made chaff cutter and stall-feeding quite popular in these villages. As stall-feeding became popular, construction of cattle shed also became popular among nearly 70 per cent tribal dairy farmers. In addition, fodder crops had been raised by farmers (about 75 per cent) and nearly about the some percent of tribal farmers agreed that storage of fodder and forest grasses has increased. These major changes in dairy enterprise have resulted in increased in knowledge of scientific dairy farming practices among majority of farmers (nearly 60 per cent). As an indirect change, knowledge of agricultural practices among 76 per cent farmers had also increased.

Thus employment opportunities opened up as perceived by about nearly three fourths of tribal villagers. Indeed, milk has brought prosperity to these villages. Their farm incomes have increased and the positive approach of TDCS and ITDDP had resulted in a sort of belief in government functionaries. More than half of the tribal villagers now opine on that their development orientation and participation in government-developed programmes had increased.

With increases in income of tribal dairy farmers a few significant changes have occurred in their living standards-especially in their consumption pattern, expenditure pattern and their orientation to progress and growth including health and education.

With regard to their consumption pattern, consumption of oil, milk vegetables, pulses and sugar had increased in greater number of families; consumption of rice and wheat was marginally increased.

There was also observed a significant change in their orientation toward modern health practices. About 40 per cent tribal villagers opined that preventive measures taken by people against certain diseases became popular. Similarly about 44 per cent tribal dairy farmers had said that the medical expenses of family members had increased. Another significant change was found consulting doctor at initial stage of illness of family members became a regular practice in atleast 37 per cent of tribal families. This shows that tribal people were becoming more health-conscious and were ready to resort to modern medical treatment instead of relying on the local vaidhya or home remedies.

In addition to health, education was also found to be an important aspect of tribal lives. Now about 65 per cent of tribal families had started sending their sons as well as daughters to schools. This was a ray of hop among the tribal people that they had accepted education as an important factor for growth and progress. Thus increased incomes had also resulted in some positive changes in tribal society.

Coming to spending their increased incomes on items like houses, clothes, ornaments, furniture and consumers goods, the picture was a little different. About 52 per cent tribal dairy farmers had invested their money on construction of new houses and in renovating their old houses. Nearly fifty per cent farmer had spent their money in purchasing silver and gold ornaments, while more than 50 per cent had bought more garments for their family. Only 28 per cent of farmers had observed that the expenditure on marriage ceremones had increased. Nearly 70 per cent farmers had opined that these changes were due to increase in urban contact while nearly 60 per cent observed that the life style of tribal families had changed very much and consumerism and material possession had increased. In some families (nearly 65 per cent) , thrift habit was seen to increase. Many tribal families had been found to develop an orientation for saving for future, which was usually contrary to their nature and behaviour. This may be seen as a direct reflection of another major significant change that occurred in the tribal society after the introduction of ITDDP in these villages.

And that was the major shift of the tribal economy from barter system to money currency system as has been observed by nearly 90 per cent of tribal dairy farmers.

Thus, these socio-economic changes had been observed and documented in this section, which revealed fascinating changes in the tribal economy, tribal food habits an their orientation towards many things in life including, education, health and modern dairy and agricultural technologies.

Section VII. Factors Affecting Knowledge and Adoption of Improved Dairy Production Technologies, Milk Production and Sale of Milk to Dairy co-operatives

It has been assumed in the study that the final tangible impact of ITDDP would reflect in the total milk procurement by the MPCDF Dairies. This can be seen as a direct result of total milk sale done by beneficiary diary farmers, which is gain, a result of increase in total milk production in the dairy units of tribal people. It has been again assumed that the increase in total milk production can be seen as a direct result of increased extent of adoption of improved dairy production technologies which again assumed to dependent on increased knowledge of improved dairy production technologies. Thus these four variables are the dependent variables and the factors affecting these four variables were analysed using correlation and multiple regression analysis.

7.1 Knowledge of Dairy Production Technologies

A respondent's level of knowledge of dairy production technologies on the components of breeding feeding, healthy care and dairy management was computed for each respondent. Then an effort has been made to find out the possible association between the socio-personal, socio-physiological and communication variables with the level of knowledge of dairy production technologies, and the data are presented in Table 4.7.1.

An revealed from the table the correlation coefficient of all variables with level of knowledge of dairy production technologies were computed separately for 100 cases of beneficiary farmers, 100 cases of non-beneficiary farmers and 200 case of all respondents.

Beneficiaries. The level of knowledge of dairy production technologies of beneficiaries was found to be strongly and positively associated with family type, housing, material possession, occupation, farm size, annual family income, social participation, extension contact, mass media exposure, extent of adoption of dairy production technologies, and milk production. It was significant at 0.01 level of probability. But the association of level of knowledge of dairy production technologies with education and family size was significant at 0.05 level of probability. Age, herd size, credit orientation and milk sale were found to be not associated at all.

Non-beneficiaries. The level of knowledge of dairy production technologies of non-beneficiaries was found to be positively associated with family type, material possession, occupation, farm size, annual family income, social participation, extension contact, mass media exposure, extent of adoption and milk production. Age, education, family size housing, herd size, credit orientation and milk sale were not associated with the level of non-beneficiaries.

Total respondents. All the variables except family size and housing were found to be associated with the level of knowledge of pooled respondents. Only one variable showed negative association ie.., age thereby meaning that the level of knowledge was found be more among the younger respondents of the sample.

Thus, material possession, annual family income, social participation, extension contact, mass media exposure, and milk production were found to be strongly associated with level of knowledge of all the categories of respondents.

Multiple Regression Analysis

The correlation analysis would merely give a idea about the association of independent variables with the dependent variables. In order to assess the contribution of each independent variable to the prediction of dependent variable, the data were adopted to regression analysis. In this study, knowledge was assumed as one dependent variable, which was regressed with all independent variables, and this was done three times for 100 cases of beneficiaries, 100 cases of non-beneficiaries and 200 cases of pooled total respondents. The data are presented in table 4.7.2 through 4.7.4.

Beneficiaries. It may be seen from Table 4.7.2 that all the selected variables explained to the extent of 72.99 per cent of variation in the level of knowledge of beneficiaries on the dairy production technologies. F ratio was found to be significant at 1485 degree of freedom. The statistical analysis thus indicated that all the selected variables taken together explained a highly significant amount of variation in the level of knowledge of beneficiary farmers.

Out of all the selected variables fitted in the multiple regression analysis only two variables, namely, occupation and extension contact contributed significantly to the prediction of level of knowledge of beneficiary farmers.

A tribal farmers who has taken up farming and dairying as his primary occupation would have developed the level of knowledge either on his own through experience the years or through educational activities of ITDDP. The fact that extension agency contact of beneficiary farmers has contributed significantly to be prediction of level of knowledge of beneficiary farmers has been proved empirically again.

Non-beneficiaries. As can be seen from Table 4.7.3, the variation in the level of knowledge of non-beneficiary farmers was explained by all the selected variables to the extent of 87.12 per cent. F ratio was found to be significant at 14, 85 degree of freedom. Though a highly significant amount of variation in level of knowledge of dairy production technologies of non-beneficiary farmers has been explained, through this statistical analysis, none of the selected variables could contribute significantly to the prediction of level of knowledge of non-beneficiaries.

Indeed, the level of knowledge of non-beneficiaries was very low, but the variation was found to be not resulting due to significant contribution of any of the independent variables

Total respondents. It may be seen from Table 4.7.3 that a very significant amount of variation in the level of knowledge of all respondents (87.49 per cent) has been explained by all the selected independent variables. F ratio was found significant at 14185 degree of freedom. But the two variables -occupation and extent contact had contributed significantly to the prediction of level of knowledge of all respondents under study.

7.2 Extent of Adoption of Dairy Production Technologies

Extents of adoption scores for each farmer were computed by adding up the scores on the components of breeding feeding, health care and dairy management. Then an effort has been made to find out the possible association between the socio-personal, socio-psychological and communication variables with the level of knowledge of dairy production technologies, and the data are presented in Table 4.7.5.

Beneficiaries. The extent of adoption of dairy production technologies of beneficiaries was found to be positively associated with education, family type, family size, housing, material possession, occupation, farm size, annual family income, social participation, extensions contact, mass media exposure, milk production and milk sale. Among the variables found to be not associated with extent of adoption were age, herd size and credit orientation.

Non-beneficiaries. The extent of adoption of dairy production technologies of non-beneficiary tribal farmers was found to be positively associated with family type, farm size, annual family income social participation, extension contact, and mass media exposure and milk production. Those variables not associated with extent of adoption were age, education family size, housing, material possession, occupation, herd size, credit orientation and milk sale.

Total respondents. All the variables except age and family size were found to be associated with the extent of adoption of dairy production technologies.

Thus, material possession, social participation extent contact and mass media exposure were found to be strongly associated with extent of adoption of dairy production technologies among all the category of tribal farmers respondents.

Multiple Regression Anlaysis

The correlation analysis may give the direction of association or non-association between dependent and independent variables. But in order to assess the contribution of each independent variable to the prediction of dependent variable, the data need to be adopted to regression analysis. This was done in this study taking extent of adoption of dairy production technologies and the data are presented in tables' 4.7.6 through 4.7.8

Beneficiaries. It may be seen from the table 4.7.6 that all the selected variables explained to the extent of 63.06 per cent variation in the extent of adoption of dairy production technologies. F ratio was found to be significant at 14, 85 degree of freedom. The statistical analysis thus indicated that all the selected variables taken together explained a highly significant amount of variation in the extent of adoption by beneficiaries.

Out of all the selected variables fitted in the multiple regression analysis only one variable, viz., level of knowledge of dairy production technologies contributed significantly to be prediction of extent of adoption of beneficiary farmers.

Tribal dairy farmers who were found to adopt many of the dairy production technologies would definitely possess adequate knowledge of these dairy production technologies. The extension agency contact and mass media exposure were found to have contributed to the prediction of knowledge of dairy production technologies. And the level of knowledge had contributed to the prediction of extent of adoption by the beneficiaries of ITDDP.

Non-beneficiaries. As can be seen from the table 4.7.7 the variation in the extent of adoption of non-beneficiary farmers was explained by all the selected variables to the extent of 83.80 per cent. F ratio was found to be significant at 13, 86 degree of freedom. Though a highly significant amount of variation in the extent of adoption of dairy production technologies by the non-beneficiaries has been explained, through this statistical analysis, only one of the selected variables - age of the non-beneficiary respondents had contributed significantly to the prediction of extent of adoption of non-beneficiaries.

Indeed, the extent of adoption of dairy production technologies of non-beneficiaries was very low, but the variation was found to be not resulting due to the contribution of any of the significant variables other than age of respondent.

Total respondents. It may be seen from the table 4.7.8, that a very significant amount of variation in the extent of adoption of dairy production technologies by all the respondents (82.10 per cent) has been explained by all the selected variables. F ratio was found significant at 14,185 degrees of freedom. Only are variable the knowledge of dairy production technologies contributed significantly to the prediction of extent of adoption of dairy production technologies by all respondents.

7.3 Milk Production

Milk production has been operationalised as the total milk produced in the dairy unit of the tribal dairy farmer respondent on the day prior to the day of investigation. The total number of litres of milk was taken as a measure and its was put through correlation analysis to find out the relationship of milk production with socio-personal, socio-psychological and communication variables. The data are presented in Table 4.7.9

Beneficiaries. Milk production in dairy units of beneficiaries of ITDDP was found to be positively associated with family type, material possession, farm size, herd size, annual family income, social participation, extension contact, mass media exposure, level of knowledge of dairy production technologies and extent of adoption of dairy production technologies. Milk production in dairy units of beneficiary tribal dairy farmers was no associated with age, education, family size, housing, occupation, credit orientation and milk sale.

Non-beneficiaries. Milk production in the dairy units of non-beneficiary tribal dairy farmers was found to be associated with all the variables except age, family size, occupation, and credit orientation and milk sale.

Total Respondents. Milk production in the dairy units of all respondents was associated all the variables except family size; age of respondents was negatively associated with milk production.

Multiple Regression Analysis

An attempt has been made, through multiple regression analysis, to assess the contribution of independent variables to the prediction of dependent variable-milk production in the dairy units of respondent farmers. The data thus analyzed are presented in table 4.7.10 through 4.7.12.

Beneficiaries. It may be seen from Table 4.7.10, that all the selected variables explained to the extent of 67.50 per cent of variables in the total milk production of beneficiaries F ratio was found to be significant 15,84 degree of freedom. The statistical analysis this indicated that all the selected variables taken together explained a highly significant amount of variation in the total milk production of beneficiary tribal dairy farmers.

Out of all the selected variables fitted in the multiple regression analysis only four variable, namely family type, family size, herd size and material possession contributed significantly to the prediction of milk production of beneficiary farmers.

Non-beneficiaries. As can be seen from Table 4.7.11 the variation in the milk production in the dairy units of non-beneficiaries was explained by all the selected variables to the extent of 72.53 per cent. F ratio was significant at 15, 84 degrees of freedom. The statistical analysis this indicated that all the selected variables taken together explained a highly significant amount of variation in the total milk production of non-beneficiaries.

Out of all the selected variables fitted in the multiple regression analysis only five variables, namely housing, farm size, herd size, annual family income and material possession.

Total respondents. It may be seen from the table 4.7.12, that a very significant amount of variation in the extent of adoption of dairy production technologies by all the respondents was explained by all the selected variables (71.50 per cent). F ratio was found significant at 15,184 degrees of freedom. Among the variables age, family type, family size, social participation, farm size, herd size, annual family income, and knowledge of dairy production technologies contributed significantly to the prediction of milk production of respondents under study.

7.4 Milk Sale

Milk sale has been oprationalised as the total milk (in litres) sold by each respondent to the TDCS on the day prior to the investigation; correlation analysis was used to find out the relationship of milk sale with socio-personal socio-psychological and communication variables. The data are presented in Table 4.7.13.

Beneficiaries: The beneficiary tribal dairy farmers were the members of TDCS in their villages and they sell milk to it. Milk sale was found to be positively associated with only a few variables included in the study: material possession, extension contact and mass media exposure. The correlation coefficients were significant at 0.05 level of probability.

Non-beneficiary: Some of the non-beneficiary tribal dairy farmers, though not being members of TDCS, sold milk to TDCS in their villages. Their milk sale was found to be associated with their level of education and farm size. None of other variables were found to be associated.

Total respondents: Milk sale of all respondents was found to be associated with many variables - age (negatively) education, housing, material possession, herd size, annual family income, social participation, credit orientation, extension contact, mass media exposure, knowledge of dairy production technologies, extent of adoption of dairy production technologies and milk production.

Multiple Regression Analysis

In order to assess the contribution of each independent variable to the prediction of dependent variable, the data were adopted to regression analysis. In this study, milk sale by beneficiaries was assumed as one of the four dependent variables, which was regressed with all the independent variables. Other three dependent variables were also included in the regression equation. This analysis was done for 100 cases of beneficiaries only.

It may be seen from Table 4.7.14, that all the selected variables explained to the extent of 26.67 per cent of variables in the milk sale to TDCS by beneficiaries. F ratio was found to be non-significant. The statistical analysis this indicated that all the selected variables taken together explained a very low amount of variation in the milk sale by beneficiary.

Out of all the selected variables fitted in the multiple regression analysis only four variables, namely farm size, annual family income, credit orientation and total milk production.

Section VIII. Problems Faced Beneficiary Farmers and Officials of ITDDP

4.8.1 Problems Faced by The Beneficiary Tribal Dairy Farmers

Beneficiary tribal dairy farmers were found to face problems in participating in the integrated tribal dairy development programme (ITDDP) of the government of Madhya Pradesh. Different levels of milk producers have stated these problems and the results are presented in Table 4.8.1.

The milk producers were grouped into three categories based on their level of milk production as low level milk producers (producing less than 8 liters daily), medium level milk producers (producing milk between 9 and 19 liters daily) and high level milk producers (producing more than 20 liters of milk daily). These three groups of tribal farmers had different perception of the problems they faced. Further, for easy understanding these problems were also classified, economic problems and organisation problems, which were discussed in detail in the following pages.

A. Socio -personal Problems

One major problem faced by tribal farmers is coming from the traditional cultural setting of their tribal society. Mostly, milk is perceived as a sacred gift of God to Mother Cow for consumption by the calf. So, milk consumption in tribal society is often found to be very low, as it is considered a food for the calf of the cow or buffalo and not meant for human consumption. So sale of milk is also considered a taboo, as it is perceived a crime against the holy cow and Mother Nature. So there is a prejudice against sale of milk. A strong misconception prevailed among.

The tribal people, mostly among medium level milk procedures, that sale of milk is a sign of poverty and hence a sign of lower socio-economic status. This can be seen among 84 per cent of all tribal respondents with only 50 per cent of high-level milk producer-respondents having no such misconception. Next major problem faced by TDCS members was the existence of milk vendors and contractors in the village operating against the interests of promotion of tribal dairy development programme in these villages. These milk vendors usually adopt such illegal practices as enticing the tribal members with so-called soft-loans for purchasing milk animals and usually for consumption expenditure like wedding, betrothal and Mundan ceremonies in the village.

In addition, a very strong social problem of these tribal villages is the existence of groupism and factionalism, which thwarts the process of cooperation among villagers. These groups spread rumours and ideological extreme thoughts among people that perpetuate division in the peace-loving tribal societies. In addition, some of the member farmers try to exploit others and generally most of the farmers are prejudiced that office bearrs of TDCS were often dialoyal to other fellow members.

All these social and personal problems as perceived by individual tribal farmers actually get accentuated due to diffusion of these thoughts and perceptions among the tribal society, thereby further aggravating the problems.

B. Economic Problems

Most of the tribal farmers who were the members of TDCS of these villages perceived that the TDCS was not really helping the farmers in their socio-economic upliftment. The local TDCS was not providing any advance facility to the tribal farmers. This was in contrast to the general practice of advancing loans by the milk vendors and slowly cutting off the payment due when milk is sold daily. Milk vendors also say that the advance payment is interest free but the sale price of milk per litre is a few paise, usually 25 paise to 50 paise, lower than the usual rate. This practice by milk vendors seems to be attractive to these poor tribal farmers and so the major problem as faced by 95 per cent of farmers is that TDCS is not giving any advance facility to its members. Delayed payment of TDCS is another associated problem.

In addition, milk vendors raise the milk sale price in different seasons while milk sale price given by TDCS was perceived by as many as 91 per cent farmers as lower. Milk venders usually pay high price to procure more milk for their customers in the lean season (say summers) when the milk supply is very low and demand is high. But TDCS gives very low price in comparison. In addition, due to improper fat and SNF testing procedure, the milk producers were found to be not getting the real sale price due to them from the TDC society.

Tribal farmers also perceived that scarcity of green fodder for their milch animals as the most important problem (which was ranked as First) in their dairy development programme. Scarcity of green fodder was aggravated by the introduction of exotic cross-breds in the tribal villages. This was also aggravated by the existence of small land holdings among the low and medium level milk procedures who were found to be not able to allot a piece of land for legume fodders or grasses. Grazing lands were also found to be shrinking in these villages, while reserve forests would not allow cattle grazing. Paddy straw was found to be the only source of fodder for the milch animals. Use of balanced nutrition mixtures concentrates and oil cakes was also low as the purchasing power of these tribal people was found to be quite lower.

Due to these factors, tribal member farmers were found to perceive that milk production was usually a costly proposition. With lower milk sale price offered by TDCS this was perceived as a low profitable enterprise. Hence the economic problems were found to be quite related to one another and aggravating the already grave situation of these tribal farmers.

C. Organisational problems

In the light of the socio-personal and economic problems as perceived by different levels of milk producers it becames quite evident efficient running of the TDCS for solving the problems of tribal farmers can not be over emphasized. But, on the contrary, the tribal farmers perceived a few significant problems in the way the TDCS is being organised, managed and supervised by the TDCS officials and office bearer tribal farmers.

Among the problems faced by the farmers, the TDCS was found to be not responding to the actual needs of tribal dairy farmers. The first major problem is that TDCS of the village was not providing any timely veterinary services. Even delayed veterinary aid was not sufficient enough thereby resulting in high mortality rate among milch animals. Due to lack of adequate health care facilities, the animals usually fall sick and their milk production gets adversely affected. Breed improvement through artificial insemination techniques was also found to be lacking.

In addition, unreliable fat testing procedures followed by TDCS officials was perceived as the most important (ranked second) problem faced by the tribal dairy farmers. Timely vaccination was found to be not at all in practice. The farmer members also perceived poor quality of inputs-usually, fodder seeds, feed concentrates, vaccines and artificial insemination and veterinary medicines and services as the major problems.

Delayed payment of TDCS to its tribal dairy farmers was a major problem among all low level milk producers, and among 80 per cent of medium level milk producers and only among 40 per cent of high level milk producers. Though high-level milk producers can withstand delayed payment, small and medium level tribal farmers faced acute shortage of money to meet their daily needs. Hence these farmers perceived this problem differently.

Lastly, TDCS's of the tribal village were found to be not actively making any efforts to promote milk production by the tribal dairy farmers. Usually, no extension services, training programmes on dairy technology and on efficient management practices for running TDCS's were being taken up by TDCS. The TDCS's were also not found to hold any general body meetings and not disturbuting any bonus among its members except in Jabhua district. There was found to be a general apathy among the members and a few influential persons manage the TDCS to their advantage and benefit. People's participation was found to be quite minimal.

Thus the problems faced by the tribal dairy farmers centred around adequate milk sale price, efficient running of TDCS's provision of essential services and inputs by TDCS and timely payment of money due to them. The TDCS at district level need to look into these problems of TDCS at village level.

4.8.2. Problem Faced by the Officials in Execution of the Inlagrated Tribal Dairy Development Programme (ITDDP)

The officials working in the ITDDP of the government of Madhya Pradesh had identified a few problems that were coming in the way of efficient running of the activities of the dairy development programme. These problems had been classified into three groups viz., A) Farmers ignorance related problems, B) TDCS working related problems and C) ITDDP administration related problems. The affirmative responses to these problems by the officials were presented in Table 4.8.2.

The results presented in the table are quite self-explanatory with each problems being ranked on maximum reposes. These are discussed in detail below.

A. Farmer's Ignorance Related Problems

The efficient functioning of tribal dairy cooperative society (TDCS) at village level in a very crucial factor for the success of ITDDP at district and state level. TDCS is the basic unit of the whole programmes of dairy development. The again depends on the active participation of the local tribal people. Since the tribal people in general were found to perceive that a few vested interests and influential people had taken charge of the society affairs, tribal dairy farmer's participation and involvement in decision making was very poor. This may also be due to the general perception that some executive members were not loyal to the society and not committed to the goals of ITDDP. Thus, many tribal people were found to disown their own TDCS at village level. These sets of problems of farmer's ignorance were found to be aggravating the problems of officials working at the village level.

B. TDCS Working Related Problems

In extension of the problems related to farmer's ignorance a few problems also have been identified by the officials of ITDDP in running the TDCS efficiently at village level. TDCS at village level seem to be suffering form three pronged problems - one of problems connected to groupism and nepotism of executive members coupled with frequent interference by politicians in day-to day affiars of TDCS. Another set of issues revolve around payment of dues to milk producers on time. The usual problem was found to be delayed payment because of delayed release of payment form the milk union at district level. The third set of problems seem to be quite serious as the technical expertise was not available and timely help may not reach the beneficiary tribal dairy farmers in times of crises such as sudden deterioration of health of milch animals, irregular supply of technical input, etc. In addition, shortage of equipment of TDCS centre aggravates the problems of officials ITDDP in running the TDCS efficiently.

C. ITDDP Administration Related Problems

The officials also aired few problems that need to be tackled at the district and state headquarters. One major problems experienced by officials was about insufficient finance from government coupled with high cost of transportation. This may be the reason for the delayed release of payment due to TDCS by the district level officials. In covering a large area of jurisdiction, which might be affecting their supervision? Frequent transfer of staff was another problems, which may also affect the working in ITDDP.

Thus these problems would bring to light the possible areas of intervention and remedial measures for efficient execution of the integrated tribal dairy development programme in the tribal areas of the state.

Section IX: Members Suggestion for Smooth Functioning of TDCS

A part of the study, members were also asked to give their suggestion for smooth functioning of TDCS which were complied and presented in Table 4.9.1. The cursory look at the contents of the table reveal that the suggestion as provided by the members can be classified into four major issues viz., sale price of milk, technical services expected from society, credit facilities from society and efficient management controls on running of society.

It has been observed that in most of the TDCS under the study area, members were not getting remunerative prices for their milk. Individual procedure is not getting appropriate prices computing with the quality (fat and SNF content) of their milk. Instead they are getting a price, which has been fixed on the whole pool of milk collected from the village. Most of the members suggested that the milk rate (sale price) need to be increased and should be calculated on the basis of fat and SNF content of mil sold by individual milk producer. Another major suggestion (which was ranked first) was on timely payment of money due to the milk producers.

It was also observed that the milk sale price as fixed by the chilling plant from the calculation of fat and SNF content of whole pool of milk from a village is not announced, usually, among the milk producer members of the society. These issues being technical and tribal milk producers being illiterate and ignorant usually be kept away for the knowledge of tribal people by the educated society office bearers.

The second major issue is provision of technical services to the tribal milk producers. The suggestions made by the members usually were on the society's initiative to provide all types of veterinary and health care service to the illiterate tribal people. Mortality rate among milch animals was found to be usually high as many tribal people are poor and ignorant about health care practices. In addition, the members also sought the help of the society to provide timely vaccination to thwart the break of an epidemic of cattle disease usually HSBQ and Foot and Mouth disease away cattle and buffaloes.

The third issue of member's suggestion revolves around credit facilities. Since the tribal people are resource-poor, they sought the help of the society in providing credit facilities for the purchase of milch animals and also for construction of a cattle shed for efficient livestock management. In addition, to supplement animal nutrition, members also suggested that society should provide timely and adequate supply of quality fixed and fodder for better animal nutrition, an subsidiesed rates. This will definitely help in the increased milk production and better health care of animals.

The fourth issue of member's suggestion was an more efficient management control mechanism to control the society officials. Most of the tribal members felt that the society officials do not dinelge useful technical information to the members and also often resort to exploitative practices and rob the ignorant tribal milk producers of their due price of milk based on actual fat content and actual SNF content. This was due to the fact that the tribal people are mostly illiterate and ignorant lot. But it is observed from the table this suggestion occupied last rank with only 56 per cent people voiced their concern on control mechanism. Here, an attempt need also be made on educating the tribal people on technical issues of fat and SNF content of milk, measurement of testing procedures, calculation of rate (sale price) of milk and also an the maintenance of records calculation of annual balance sheet, and lastly distraction of profit-related bonus to members, etc.

Thus the suggestions made by the members were also appropriate, relevant and genuine. This also had shown how concerned the tribal people are for better management and continuous running of TDCS in their village.

Section X. Strategy of Strengthening Dairy Development Programme in Tribal Areas

This study on impact to ITDDP on tribal people has brought out clearly some key issue, if addressed well and timely, would strengthen the dairy development programmes in tribal areas. A strategy needs to be planned to address the following key issues:

(a) Educational of farmers for active participation
(b) Building strong institution that can sustain
(c) Fixing reasonable price of milk being supplied to TDCS
(d) Massive emphasis on cattle bred
(e) Provision of veterinary services for each cluster of villages

(f) Infrastructure development including transport facilities

(g) Provision of green fodder banks and pastures management

h) Special package for tribal people

(a) Education of Farmers for Active Participation

* This is the most important of all the issues. Tribal people are in general ignorant, backward and conservative in their outlook. They possess a lot of prejudices and misconception on the sale of milk and believe in customers and ritual that promote dogmatic fatalistic orientation among them. Educational opportunities need to be exploited so that they develop a modern scientific orientation and grow out of superstitions.

It has been found in the study that education, extension contact and mass media exposure were playing a positive role in creating a critical awareness among the tribals and helping them to increase their share of benefits from the village level TDCS. Special training camps may be organised in the village to educate farmers on the improved dairy production technologies. The tribal peoples role and responsibility in running the TDCS successfully and mechanism for encouraging active participation and involvement need to be addressed in such camps. Educational component of veterinary advisory services needs to be enhanced in the extension activities of ITDDP.

(b) Building Strong Institution that can Sustain

It has been seen that, given a chance, tribal people can excel, as was seen in the five villages of Jhabua district of study. The tribal people have accepted the TDCS and embraced it as an important part of their tribal culture. They were found to exhibit feelings of ownership and were taking all necessary measures for nurturing it and sustaining it.

Such cooperative ventures have been seen as modern day temples of progress. Such economic institutions bringing about economic independence among the poor tribals need to be further strengthened. The tribal people, having seen the success of the cooperative TDCS in their villages were encouraged to participate in the mainstream of national development. This success has to be translated into a strategy of building. Cooperative spirit among the tribal people. To enable this happen, strong institutional building activities need to be incorporated in the strategy to transform tribal people and their lives. Existing TDCSs need to be given new orientation and an effort has to be done to develop mutually acceptable na.. in the society and strict adherence to the norms be practiced and encouraged. Care should be taken to see that the TDCSs flourish and diversify into other related areas of enterprise where tribal people get the maximum benefit.

At the village level, TDCS need to be made truly democratic. It left to the management by the traditional leaders, it may soon fall sick as peculiar caste politics and group dynamics start over powering and stifling this new economic institution in the village. Factionalism and groupism has to be kept away from this institution. Favouritism and nepotism in the management of TDCS has to be curtailed and new hope is instilled among members through generation of collective responsibility and accountability among members and transparency in its operations.

Members need to be provided critical awareness on the various possible benefits one may accrue from being a member of TDCS. When these benefits are properly and equitably distributed among all members, members would develop a kind of faith in institutions of government and start participating in decision-making, assume ownership of such institution to sustain, survive and serve one and all equally.

(c) Fixing Reasonable Price of Milk being Supplied to TDCS

It has been observed in the study that there appeared many misunderstandings about milk price being fixed by the district milk producers cooperative union. A lot of mistrust was being generated among the tribal people. Milk price was being fixed on the quality of pooled milk of the whole village and not on the basis of individual suppliers milk quality. No incentives were being provide for supplying better quality of milk by individual suppliers.

This has become a key issue reflecting on the health of the TDCS. Milk price need to be fixed on the basis of fat and SNF content of milk supplied by each members and not on the pooled milk. In addition, a provision f subsidy be made to enable fixing a slightly higher milk procurement price for the tribal areas in order to encourage tribal dairy enterprises of members and also to enable TDCS compete with the local milk vendors.

(d) Massive Emphasis on Cattle Breed Improvement

A really massive emphasis needs to be given on cattle breed improvement in the tribal areas. Since the cattle in these areas are very low productive in nature, new breeds like Jersey and Holstein Freisian may be used in cross-breeding programme through large scale artificial insemination and through provision of live bulls for natural crossing. Local bulls of good breedings may also be provided for natural crossing in order to build a healthy herd of milch cattle in each tribal village.

(e) Provision of Veterinary Services for each Cluster of Villages

It has been found that the provision of timely help in veterinary aid to the needy farmers of the remote tribal areas plays a key role in the success of a TDCS in the village.

Since these tribal dairy farmers were ignorant of the new dairy production technologies especially animal health care aspects, veterinary services assume a bigger place in the strategy to transform dairy enterprises of the tribal farmers. A veterinary sub-center need to be established to cover 5-6 villages so that the breeding practices of the milch cattle and the health of animals is improved and milk procurement enhanced. At least one livestock inspector be posted at these contres who will be supported by the visiting veterinary surgeon who attends to any emergency calls made by members of TDCS. Provision of veterinary treatment, medicines, vaccines and event artificial insemination facilities be made on an assured basis to the tribal people throughout the year.

Madhuvans were found to be functioning well in some districts and they need to be reinvigorated to provide the facilities of better animal healthy care and to build a healthy improved herd in each district.

(f) Infrastructure Development Including Transport Facilities

Since these districts under study are tribal dominated areas and backward areas with high forest cover and few roads, special emphasis need to be given to infrastructure development especially road transport and communication. To reduce the high cost of transportation charges, each tribal district need to be divided into divisions and Divisional Milk Union at nearby town need toe be proposed so that milk procurement may increase.Area of jurisdiction under supervision may also become less along with operational problems. Cooperative milk union dairies and chilling centres may also be set up at one or two towns besides the one dairy already functioning at district headquarters.

Transport changes of milk were also found to be an higher sides in comparison to other regions due to lack of good roads and non-availability of private transporters on existing rates. Subsidy on diesel may be provided to attract transporter to the milk transportation business. State government can also finance rural trucks/ milk vans to the unemployed tribal youth, which will encourage transport business in the tribal community.

Provision of telecommunication facilities may be provided at village level to enable faster communication between TDCS and district milk union and apex body at the state level.

(g) Provision of Green Fodder Banks and Pastureland Management

Availability of green fodder around the year can be assured with the collaboration programme for pasture land development and fodder crop development with active involvement of all the concerned agencies like state agricultrual department, animal husbandry department, Madhya Pradesh Dairy Cooperative Federation, state forest department, wasteland development boards, state agricultural universities, Indian Institute of Fodder Crops and Grasslands

Research Institute of ICAR located at Hansi, Uttar Pradesh, etc. With the collective efforts of these agencies wastelands, ravines, reiver belts, forestlands, open pasturelands, hillsides, panchayat, Gram Sabha common land, etc. can be utilised as fodder resources by transplanting range grasses mixed with legume grasses.

A fodder bank can be established at the Tribal Dairy Cooperative Society of the village level. These banks can procure, process, enrich, conserve the surplus fodder in the season and provide the fodder to TDCS members during periods of fodder shortage.

The village common lands and nearby forest pastureland may also be managed by TDCS through rotation grazing techniques so that all the milch cattle and other livestock get adequate and healthy nutrition.

(h) Specific Package for Tribal People

With the success of dairy enterprises of small individual farmers in the villages of better regions, the tribal people were found to lag behind. SO it is suggested that a special package deal for the tribal people may be given, which include better milk price, better facilities at veterinary sub-centres and subsidised service of transport and technical inputs and services. Even the area of jurisdiction of operations and staff may be reduced as these tribal districts cover larger area.

Thus the strategy had addressed all the key issues and if the state government and the Madhya

Pradesh Dairy Cooperative Federation takes note of the suggested strategy dairy development in tribal areas would improve in leaps and bounds.

Summary and Conclusion

Animal husbandry esssential and well-integrated sub-system of Indian agriculture has been playing a vital role in supplementing the livelihoods of weaker section of our society.

A single successful cooperation endeavor in Kheda district of Gujrat. Which later come to be know a AMUL, had brought about need hope in modern dairy cooperative movement in India. Then the National Dairy Development Board had been set upto to promote dairy cooperations in seventeen promisinng. " Milk sheds' in ten states and to build four metropolitan dairies (Kurin, 1999). Thus began the two large sale programmes called operation flood II and I, which brought about white revolution in India.

In Madhya Pradesh, Madhya Pradesh Dairy cooperative Federation, MPAVAVN, NSFDC along with collaboration with NDDB had started ITDDP in some selected tribal districts of Madhya Pradesh, with an overall objective of promoting sustainable livelihoods for tribal people through developing tribal dairy cooperative societies (TDCSs). The key research issue here was to find the impact of these efforts by Madhya Pradesh Dairy cooperative would enable the government machinery to strengthen the initiatives and the sturctures of development of tribal people. So with the overall objective of assessing dairy cooperatives in the tribal bell of Madhya Pradesh and to know its impact an tribal lives, a study entitled " A Critical study and the Impact of Dairy Development Programmes on the Tribals of Madhya Pradesh with special reference to Dairy cooperatives" was planned with the following specific objective:

Methodology

This study has been carried out the tribal belt of Madhya Pradesh. Out of the 13 tribal districts, five districts *viz.,* Mandla, Sarguja, Rai, Bastar and Jhabua were selected. From each district, five villages were selected. From each village, one TDCS were selected. 25 TDCSs were selected.

From each TDCS, eight tribal farmers (4 beneficiaries and 4 non-beneficiaries) were selected. In total 200 farmers were selected as respondents of the study. In addition 25 officials of ITDDP working in TDCS, DMU of MPDCF were selected for study.

An ex-post facto research design was followed and the farmers and officials were interviewed to collect data on various aspects of impact of ITDDP o their lives. Variables included in the study are: socio-personal characteristics of tribal farmer respondents including age, education, family type, family size, housing, material possession, occupation, farm size, herd size, annual family income, social participation, credit orientation and knowledge about dairy production technology, communication variables including extension contact and mass media exposure, and dependent variables including extent of adoption of dairy production technology, milk production and milk sale.

Major Findings

Section I : Integrated Tribal Dairy Development Programme: Genesis Activities and TDCS

Integrated Tribal Dairy Development (ITDDP) was started in 10 selected tribal districts of Madhya Pradesh. This study covered five districts in the state. District milk union at each district headquarters coordinates working of the tribal dairy cooperative societies in village. Milk is collected from each village and sent to district milk union dairy where it is pasteurised processed and sent to urban areas for sale to consumers.

The officials at the district level provide support to the TDCS in terms of veterinary treatment to animal, providing fodder seed, and general supervision in running the TDCS in the villages and transportation of milk to the district milk union dairy on a daily basis. They provide adequate training to a selected youth of the village and appoint him a secretary of each TDCS who is paid by the revenue generated in the TDCS.

The success of each TDCS depends on the way it is run by the secretary TDCS and patronized by the members. Some societies were found to be running well, processing milk in good quantity and earning profits. The success of each TDCS also depended on the trust and confidence it enjoyed among the villagers.

Section II: Profile of Respondents

The respondents were tribal dairy farmers living in the five selected villages in each of the five selected districts of the tribal belt of Madhya Pradesh. Respondents included were the beneficiaries-members of TDCS who enjoyed the benefits of ITDDP and non-beneficiaries-non-members who did into enjoy the benefits of ITDDP. The profiles of these two categories of respondents were drawn and presented below:

Beneficiaries. Thus the average profile of respondents can be drawn as thus: Beneficiary tribal dairy farmer respondents appear to middle aged, educated upto middle school level, living in a nuclear family with medium size of family in a kachha house and possessing more than six items of farm equipment and household goods. The average beneficiary farmers has farming and dairying as the principal occupation, possessing about six acres of land on an average with cattle herd size of six animal on his farm, and earning an average annual family income of about Rs. 30000 only. He appears to be actively participating in more than one social organisation both at village and block level and usually taking loans from local moneylenders in the village. He appears to be moderately high frequency of contact with extension agencies and having better than medium level of exposure to mass media. He was found to posses moderate level of knowledge and so also had moderate extent of adoption of dairy production technologies. Though he produces more than 9 litres of milk on an average, he was found to sell 3 litres of milk only to TDCS in his village.

Non beneficiaries. On the contrary, the non-beneficiary tribal dairy farmers respondent appear to be old in age, educated upto primary school level, living in a nuclear family with large size of family in a kachha house and possessing less then five items of farm equipment and household goods. The average non-beneficiary farmers has farming and dairying as the primary occupation, possessing about five acres of land on an average with cattle herd size of four animal on his farm, and earning an average annual family income of about Rs. 25000 only. The non-beneficiary tribal farmers appear to be not actively participating in any social organisation of the village and usually taking loans from village moneylenders. He appears to have a low frequency of contact with extension agents, and less exposure to mass media. His knowledge of improved dairy production technologies was also very low and hence lowers extent of adoption. Though he produces and 7 litres of milk per day on an average, he hardly sells any to TDCS but selling elsewhere or consuming in their large families.

Section III : Difference between beneficiaries to ITDDP and non-beneficiaries

Beneficiary respondents were found to be significantly different, on majority of variables, from non-beneficiaries, ITDDP had brought about clearly changes in the beneficiary tribal farmers on their opinion towards ITDDP, knowledge and extent of adoption of dairy production technology, total milk production and milk sale. Clear differences among the two categories of respondents was also seen on age, education, housing, material possession, herd size, social participation, credit orientation, extent contact, mass media exposure and annual family income.

Beneficiaries and non-beneficiaries were found to be similar on their family type family size, farm size and occupation.

Section IV: Impact of ITDDP on Achievement Target Indicators and Economic Performance

Impact of ITDDP was seen on five sets of target (1996, 97 to 1998-99) indicators where the rate of change over the three years period was also calculated. (a) Herd mortality indicators: Herd mortality rate and female calf mortality rate were found to be increasing rather than decreasing. This may be due to decrease in vaccination rate and veterinary treatment rate. (b) Breeding practice indicators: Breeding rate and pregnancy rate have decreased resulting in increasing number of dry animals whereby dairy in these tribal villages was adversely affected. (c) Breeding behaviour indicators: Age of first calving averaged at 61-63 months much beyond the national average of 50 months and the intercalving period was also found to fall short of national average. The performance of animal husbandry activities was found to be not successful. (d) Nutritional standard of the herd indicators: The performance on these indicators was also found to be poor and far from satisfactory levels. The situation on all the above parameter, in the two districts of Jhabua and Raigarh appeared to be better than in other three districts under study.

(e) Economics performance indicators: Members and total milk suppliers got reduced over three year period in the districts of Sarguja, Mandla and Bastar. In Jhabua district, the members and milk sellers increased. Milk procurement and net profit also showed the same trends.

The situation in Jhabua district was found to be improving over the years on all indicators whereby a ray of hope is generated among the tribal people here. This positive impact had brought about a new cycle of progress among the tribal dairy farmers of this district.

Section V: Opinion of Tribal Farmers Respondents and TDCS Officials on the ITDDP Activities

Beneficiaries of ITDDP were found to have a highly favourable opinion comapred to non-beneficiaries. Beneficiaries who had accrued many benefits from ITDDP had opined that there was a lot of improvement in knowledge and extent of adoption of dairy production technologies, animal healthy care facilities, etc. This had also resulted in positive improvement in the living standards of tribal people especially in their consumption pattern and life style. Positive consequence was also seen on tribal lives.

The officials of ITDDP and TDCS had mixed opinion on the activities of ITDDP. This may be due to some constraints they might be facing in their activities.

Section VI: Socio-economic Changes in Living Standards of Tribal People after the Introduction of ITDDP

ITDDP had brought about fascinating changes in socio-economics fabric of tribal people- in the tribal food habits, in the tribal economy and in their orientation towards many things in life including, education, health and modern dairy and agricultural technologies.

Section VII: Factors Affecting knowledge, Adoption of Dairy Production Technologies, Milk Production and Milk Sale to Dairy Cooperatives

a) Knowledge of dairy production technologies was found to be affected by only to variables - occupation and extension contact. In the case of beneficiaries, their occupation of farming and daiyring and their extension contact had contributed significantly to the prediction of their knowledge of dairy production technologies.

b) Extent of adoption of dairy farming technologies wad found to be affected by only one significant variables beneficiary's knowledge of dairy production technologies. Knowledge possessed by a tribal dairy farmer had contributed significantly to the prediction of their extent of adoption of dairy production technologies.

c) Milk production in the dairy units of tribal farmers could not be explained by the key variables of knowledge and extent of adoption of dairy production technologies. But this variables was found to be affected by variables like family type, family size, herd size, material possession, in the case of beneficiaries while it was affected by housing, farm size, herd size, annual family income and material possession.

d) Milk sale by the beneficiaries to the TDCS was also found to be not explained by the key variables of knowledge an extent of adoption of dairy production technologies. This variable was found to be affected by farm size, annual family income, credit orientation and total milk production.

Section VIII: Problems Faced by Beneficiaries and Officials of ITDDP

Beneficiaries faced a lot of problem in running the TDCS in their villages. They are

Lack of infrastructure and facilities at TDCS Groupism in the villages and abundance of milk vendors and contraction

Taboos and misconception on milk sale.

Scarcity of green fodder, drinking water and other amenities

Improper running of TDCS

Unreliable methods of fat testing at TDCS

Comparatively low milk price offered by TDCS Delayed veterinary aid in the village by TDCS

Lack of advance facility by TDCS

ITDDP officials also faced a few significant problems in the execuation of ITDDP activities

Farmers were found to be ignorant of the facilities available at TDCS

Executive members were found to be not legal to members of TDCS

Poor involvement and lack of ownership of TDCS among the tribal dairy farmers.

TDCS was into being managed well

Irregularly payment by union at district level to TDCS

Interference of politicians in day-to-day affairs of TDCS

Vast area of jurisdiction under supervision

Insufficient financial aid from government.

Section IX: Members Suggestion for Smooth Functioning of TDCS

For efficient running and smooth functioning to TDCS members of society gave a few suggestion worth mentioning here. They are

Timely and regularly payment of due by the society

Provision of veterinary services including vaccination

Provision of loan facility to purchase milch animals, and to construct cattle shed

Provision of subsidised feed and fodder by the society on credit basis

Revision of existing milk rate on the basis of fact and NSF rather than on average rate.

These suggestions appear to be reasonable and can be implemented for sustained running of TDCS in each village.

Section X: Strategy for Strengthening Dairy Development Programme in Tribal Areas

A strategy has been planned and proposed in this study to strengthen the dairy development programme in tribal areas. The key points of strategy are:

Bringing about integration of all the related department of state government with MPCDF.

Provision of enhanced financial assistance for starting new district milk union dairies and chilling centres.

Provision of funds for infrastructure development like road transport and communications.

Establishment of veterinary sub-centres for a cluster of 5-6 villages

Bibliography

Agarwal, Urmila (1977). Social consequence of technological changes in a C.D. Block, New Delhi.

Agresco Report (1973). "A study of the agricultural problems of Adivasi Farmers form Navapur Taluka of Dhulia District. Mahatama Phule Krishi Vidyapeeth, College of Agriculture, Dhulia, pp. 1-24.

Anonymous (2000). "India retains lead in milk production: *Observer*, 2 may, 2000.Awasthi, P.K., Srivastava, A. Gupta, S.K. and Atkare, P. (1986)., Integrated Rural Development Programme : Receptivity and Reaction, *Indian J. Agric. Econ.,* 41(4) : 670-671.

Banerjee, S. (1976). "A study of socio-economic and demographic factors associated among tribal farmers of Bastar district of M.P. (Published M.Sc., Thesis, Publication, Division, Haryana Agril. Univ. Hisar), C.F. Thesis Abstract, vol. II, No., 2, June, 1976.

Bapat, M.T. and Brahmbhat, D.M.(1976). Transforming Tribal Agriculture. Sardar

Patel Univ.Vallabh Vidhyanagar (Gujarat). *Arthe Vikas* 12 (2) : 74.

Barnabas, A.P. (1969). Social change in North Indian Village, *Indian Institute of Public Administration,* New Delhi.

Basu, S.K. (1975). "Tribal Indebtedness and the Wayout. *Kurukshetra,* 23: 12.

Bawajir, S.M. and Nandapurkar G.G. (1984). Developmet and standarisation of the socio-economic status scale to measure the socio-economic status of farmers. M.Sc. Thesis, M.A.U., Parbhani (M.S).

Bhati, J.P. and Swarup, R. (1974). Economic problems of Tharu Tribes. *Kurukshitra,* 23(2): 10-11.

Bhople, R.S. and Agrawal, S.S. (1987). Constraints in adoption of farm technology. Paper presented in the seminar on constraints in Transfer of Technology held at K.K.V., Dapoli, Oct 20-30,1987.

Borgohain, A and Kakoty, H.N. (1990). Correlates of adoption of animal husbandry practices by the dairy farmers of Greater Guwahati Milkshed. *Indian Psy. Review,* 35 (9-10) : 1-5.

Chahal, H.S. (1980). A study of factors affecting production of milk by cattle owners in the milk shed area of Ludhiana milk plant (Punjab). M.Sc. thesis, National Dairy Research Institute, Karnal.

Chander, S. (1970). A study of socio-economic factors affecting the adoption of artificial insemination and attitude of farmers towards the same. M.Sc. Thesis, Punjab Univ. Chandigarh.

Chattopadhyay, B. (1976). Diffusion of wheat technology in traditionally rice growing states an analysis. M.Sc. (Ag) Thesis, Indian Agricultural Research Institute, New Delhi.

Chaubey, C.L. (1972). A study of differential adoption of high yielding wheat varieties technology as related to influence by selected demographic, socio-psychological and political variables in Sehore distirt, Madhya Pradesh, Ph.D. Thesis, Indian Agricultural Reseach Institute, New Delhi.

Chaubey, K.N. (1991). A study of the differnetial relationship in decisoin making among farmers in relatin to dairy innovaitons in Allahabad District (U.P.). Ph.D. Thesis, National Dairy Research Institute, Karnal.

Chauhan, J.P.S. (1979). A study of some socio-personal economic and entrepreneurial characteristics in relation to entrepreneurial role performance of milk producers of Karnal city. M.Sc. Thesis, National Dairy Research Institute, Karnal.

Chinnaiyan, P. (1979). A study on the pattern of production and marketing of ilk in Erode Taluk, Tamilnadu, M.Sc. (Ag.) Thesis, Tamilnadu Agric. Univ. , Coimbatore.

Chitnis, D.H. (1983). A study of the technology gap in dry farming system and factors associated with technological gap. Ph.D. Thesis, Unpub. MAU Parbhani (M.S.)

Chole, R.R. (1982). Attitude of farmers towards improved agricultural technology. Agresco report, Memeographed 61-74, college of agriculture, MAU, Prabhani (M.S.).

Chopra, R.N., Chopra, I.C., Handa, K.L. and Kapoor, L.D. (1965). Indigenous Drugs of India.2nd ed. U.N.Dhar and Sons Pvt. Ltd, Calcutta, India, p.8.

Dannely, H.G. (1927). Miscellaneous Contribution Naga Medicine. *Man in India*, 7: 182-183

Dass, G.N. (1978). Whether Tribal Welfare, *Khadi Gramodyog*, 25 (5): 261.

Desai, B.M. (1976). "Formal and informal credit sources in tribal areas.". Sardar Patel Univ. Vallabh, Vidyanagar, Ahmedabad (Gujarat). *Arthe-Vikas*, 12 (2): 78.

Desai, J.C. (1976). "A wind of change Among Tribals". *Kurukshetra*, 24: 13.

Desphande, H.K. (1980). Adoption of H_4 cotton variety in Hadgaon Taluka of Nanded district. M.Sc. Thesis, MAU, Parbhani.

Dey, R.A. (1977). A study on the decision making pattern in rural families with respect to selected dairy husbandry practices in chak block of Allahabad District (U.P.). M.Sc. Thesis, NDRI, Karnal.

Dongaonkar, N.W. (1982). Opinion of the farmers regarding high yielding varieties of cotton, Jowar and wheat released by MAU, Parbhani, Agresco-report, Memographed, 12-22.

Dubey, S.N. (1971). Tribal welfare programme. A analysis of their organisation and administration, *Indian J. of Social Welfare,* Vol. 35 (4). 69-73.

Dubey, V.K., Ram, K. and Sagar, S.L. (1978). Dynamics of Dairy Co-operatives case studies, Div. of Dairy Extn., NDRI, Karnal.

Elwin, V. (1963). New Deal for Tribal India, ed. Minstry of Home Affairs, New Delhi.

FAO (1981). World Food Programme. Terminal Project Report, pp. 61-63.

Gaikward, S.P. (1985). A study of the effectiveness of information sources at persuation function in the innovation decision process. An experiment study. M.Sc. (Ag.) thesis MAU, Parbhani.

Garde, S.K. (1980). A study of technology gap of different categories of dairy farmers in the operational research project area of the National Dairy Research Institute, M.Sc. Thesis, Karnal.

Gautam, U.S. (1980). Role of aspiration and motivation in decision making with respect to adoption of dariy practices by IRDP beneficiaries of Varanasi districts (U.P.). Ph.D. thesis, NDRI, Karnal.

George, K.M. (1984). Challanges of Rural Development. *Financing Agricultural,* 16 (3) : 5-7.

Gholve, M.A., Sangle, G.K. and Chole, R.R. (1986). Media use behaviour and acceptance of modern agricultural technology by tribal farmers. Seminar on 'Role of Media in agricultural development.

Organisation by MSEE and MAU Parbhani at Aurgangabad. Mimeographed.

Ghosh, A.N. (1974). Feed and fodder, Shal we at last wake up? *Yojana,* 18 (9): 13.

Ghurye, G.S.(1957).Mahadeo Koli,Bombay,India.

Girdhar, P.N. (1967). A study of factors resisting the progress of AI in Haryana, M.Sc. Thesis HAU Campus, Hisar (Haryana).

Gite, N.R. (1980). A study of training needs of landless corssbred cattle owners under lab to land programme. M.Sc. Thesis, NDRI, Karnal.

Gopala Krishnaiah, C.H. and Pochaiah, M. (1989). Impact of primary milk producers "cooperatives Societies on beneficiaries in Nalgonda district of Andhra Pradesh. *Indian Cooperative Review,* 26 (3) : 278-282.

Grewal, R.S., Nandal, D.S. and Gupta, D.D. (1985). Impact of rural development programme on rural women in Bhiwani district of Haryana, *Indian J. Agric. Econ.,* 11 : 259.

Gulati, R.K. (1970). A Profile of Social Change among the Bhils of Western Khandesh. *Tribe,* 7 (1): 18-28.

Gupta, C.L. (1976). A study of differentail motives of dairy farmers of milk cooperative-societies of ICDP, Karnal (Haryana) towards dairy innovations. Ph.D. Thesis, NDRI Karnal.

Hansda, S. (1981). Agricultural development in Tribal Areas, in Tribal Area Development, ed. S.N. Mishra and Bhupinder Singh, Society for the study of Regional Disparities, New Delhi, 1983, pp. 21-26.

Hazarika, P. (1983). A study of correlates of knowledge and adoption behaviour of the dairy farmers under ICDP, Khanapara (Assam). M.Sc. Thesis, NDRI, Karnal.

Hirevenkenagouda, I.V., Hanumanthappa, H.S.and Jalihal (1988). Impact of dairy development on the weaker section; A Case Study. *Kurkshetra,* 36 (5): 7-11.

Hussain, S.K.M.(1950). Medicine among Gonds, Kalmas and Chenchus. *Man in India,* 30: 23-37.

Jadon, B.S. (1973). A study on the adoption of improved potato varieties and related factors in Kaira district of Gujarat state. M.Sc. Thesis, GAU, Anand.

Jain, H.C. (1986). A critical study of the impact of IRDP on agricultural sector of Jabalpur district, *Indian J.Agric. Econ.,* 41 (4) : 673-674.

Jetly, S. (1977). Modernizing Indian Peasants. A study of six villages in Eastern Uttar Pradesh, New Delhi. *Asia Educational Services*, pp. 31-70.

John, A.J. (1974). The relationship of cattle owners' pursonal characteristics with milk production in ICAR crosses breeding scheme area. M.Sc. thesis, Chalakudu, Kerala.

Kakade, S.D. (1983). Correlation of executive members' participation in management of primary milk producer's co-operative society. M.Sc. Thesis, NDRI, Karnal.

Kalappa, A. (1971). Tribal Development in Mysore". *Kurukshetra,* vol. xix, No. 5, pp. 2-4.

Kannani, D.R. (1982). "Training needs of the Tribal Farmers in relation to mazie crop at Dohad Taluka of Panchmahala District in Gujarat State. "M.Sc. (Ag.) Thesis. *Gujarat Agril. Univ.,* Anand Campus Anand.

Kaur, Jaswant (1981). A study of differential dairying knowledge and role performance of trained and untrained milk producers and their wives. M.Sc. thesis, NDRI, Karnal.

Kaushik, S.K. (1988). A study of impact of milk producers' co-operative societies on the knowledge and adoption of scientific dairy farming practices in Hisar District (Haryana). M.Sc. Thesis, NDRI, Karnal.

Kirtikar, K.R. and Basu, B.D. (1935). Indian Medicinal plants, 2nd ed. Vol.I-IV, Lalit Mohan Basu, M.B.Allahabad, India.

Kohli, P.A. (1978). Dairy cooperatives. *Indian Cooperative Review,* 15 (9): 529.

Kokate, K.D. (1980). A study of the training needs as perceived by the farmers of KVK villages (Karnal). M.Sc. Thesis, NDRI, Karnal.

Kokate, K.D. (1984). A study of dairy farming systems and technlogical gap in a tribal setting. Ph.D. Thesis, NDRI, Karnal.

Kololgi, S.D. and Anand, Usha (1985). Adoption of dairy innovations amoing selected Tibetian Rufugees of Karnataka. *Dairy Guide,* 7(6): 37-41.

Kolte, D.M. (1973). A study of the adoption of sugarcane practices and their related factors in Anand Taluka of Guajarat State, M.Sc. (Ag.) Thesis, GAU, Anand.

Kotikhane, R.R., (1986). A stuyd of the technological gap in irrigated farming system under. Purna Command area of Maharashtra state. Ph.D. Thesis, MAU, Parbhani (M.S.).

Kulkarni, R.R. (1979). An analysis of technological gap in tribal farming system. Ph.D. Thesis, MAU, Parbhani (M.S.).

Kulkarni, Satish (1999). "Can biggest milk producer become best? *Economic Times*, 20, December, 1999 p. 17.

Kurien, V. (1999). Milk, milk. Everywhere, Survey of Indian Agricultural, *The Hidnu*, 1999.

Kuttykrishanan, A.C. (1985).A poverty profile for rural Kerala. Journal of Rural Development, 4 (4) : 554-504.

Mahipal (1983). A study of socio-economic and psychological correlates in adoption of dairy innovations in ORP area of NDRI, Karnal. Ph.D. Thesis, NDRI, Karnal.*

Mahipal and Kherde, R.L. (1989). Correlates of adoption behaviour of dairy famrers. *Indian J. Dairy Sci.*, 42 (3) : 434-439.

Malik, B.S. (1978). A study of differential knowledge and adoption of animal husbandry innovations among cattle owners of Operation Research Project area under National Dairy Research Institute, M.Sc. Thesis, NDRI, Karnal.

Mathur,R.C.(1975).Jaunsar-Bawar-Rawain area in the district of Dehradun,Tehri and Uttar Kashi (UP) - A note on a survey in Integrated

TribalDevelopment Planning, ed V.R.K. Paramahansa (Hyderabad) : Nation Institute of Community Development, pp. 170.

Michael, B. (1978). Marketing in Tribal Areas. *Fertilizer News*. 23 (4) : 25.

Mitra, S. (1977). Development problems of Tribal Agriculture in India. *Geographical Society of India, Calcutta,* 39 (2) : 107-115.

Naik, T. B. (1969). Impact of education on the Bhils. Published by Research programme Committee, Planning Commission, New Delhi, India.

Nandre, K.R. (1986). A study of attitude, aspiration and reference for placement of agricultural school students in rural Maharashtra, Ph.D. Thesis, MAU, Parbhani (M.S.).

Narayanan, Rao, R. (1968). A study of differential adoption of package of practices for high yielding varieties of rice in A.P. M.Sc. (Ag.) Thesis, IARI, New Dehi.

National Commission on Agricultural (1976). A Bridged Report. Govt. of India, Ministry of Agricultural and Irrigation, New Delhi, p. 306.

Natrajan, M. S. and Channegowda, M.B. (1987). A study of knowledge and adoption behaviour of cattle owners. *Mysore J. Agric. Sci.*, 21 (3) : 354-358.

Pandit, V.K. (1981). “The constraints in transfer of wheat technology in Barwari Tribal Development Block of West Nimar District of Mahdya Pradesh, M.Sc. Thesis, Guajarat Agril. Univ. Anand (Gujarat).

Patel, G.V. (1975). Study of socio-economic characteristics of the farmers in relation to adoption of chichory cultivation in Anand Taluka in Gujarat State. Anand (Gujarat).

Patel, M.B. (1978). "An Investigation on extension works in the Integrated Tribal Development Project Area of Pamchmahala district of Gujarat state. "Unpublished M.Sc. Thesis, Gujarat Agril. Univ., Anand Campus, Anand.

Patel, M.B. (1978). "An Investigation on Extension works in the Integrated Tribal Development Project Area of Panchmahala District of Gujarat State, M.Sc. Thesis, Gujarat Agril. Univ., Anand Campus, Anand (Gujarat).

Patel, P.P. (1978). Usefulness of cotton research station. Surat as perceived by cotton growers. M.Sc. (Ag.) Thesis, Gujarat Agril. Univ., Navsari, (Gujarat).

Patil, B.P. (1981). Impact of ICDP on dairy development in milshed area of Miray (Maharastra). M.Sc. Thesis, NDRI, Karnal (Haryana).

Patnaik, N. (1972). Tribes and their development, Hyderabad (A.P.).

Pawar, S.G. (1983). A study of differential dairy development of selected states in India. Ph.D. Thesis, NDRI, Karnal (Haryana).

Prajapati, V.V. (1988). Input use behaviour of banana growers of chorayashi Taluka in

Surat district of Gujarat state. M.Sc. (Ag.) Thesis Gujarat Agril. Univ. Navsari (Guj.).

Raghav Rao, D.V. (1975). "Institutional Framework for Agricultural Development in Tribal Area". *Community Development and Panchayati Raj Digest*, 6 (3): 145-151.

Raju, D.T. and Pochaiah, M. (1991). How to popularise crossbred cows, *Yojna,* 35 (5): 25.

Ramchand, (1980). Measurement of aspiration of dairy famrers of ICDP, Karnal with projectives and non-projective technique. Ph.D. Thesis, NDRI, Karnal (Haryana).

Rangaranjan, R. (1979). A study of dairy development through milk cooperatives in Naunakal Taluk, Salem District. M.Sc. Thesis, TNAU, Coimbatore.

Rao, B.S. (1987). A study of transfer of dairy development production technologies in Chittoor district of Andhra Pradesh. Ph.D. Thesis, NDRI, Karnal (Haryana).

Ray, A.K., Atteri, B.R., Vasisth, A.K. and Ram G.S. (1981). Impact of small farmers development Agency programme on the net farm incomes labour employment pattern and off-farm income. *Financing Agriculture,* 13 (4): 10-14.

Sadamate, V.V. (1978). "A study of Tribal Farming System and Technological gaps' Unpubl. Thesis, IARI, New Delhi.

Sahay, B.N. (1969). Pragmatism in Development New Delhi: Book heive.

Sahay, K. B. (2000). "The problem of livestock population. *Tribune*, April 11, 2000, p. 10.

Saini, S.P.S. (1980). Correlates of Dairy Modernization of small and marginal dairy farmers of I.C.D.P. Ludhiana, Ph.D. Thesis, NDRI, Karnal (Haryana).

Sangle, G.K. (1980). Multivariate anaysis of technological gap in tribal farming. *Tribal Research Bulletin, Pune*, 3 (1): 15.

Sarkar, A. (1981). A study of communication behaviour of dairy famrers in relation to scientific dairy famring practices of ICDP Barsat (West Bengal) Ph.D. Thesis, NDRI, Karnal.

Sayeedi, A. G. (1983). A study of knowledge, attitude and adoption of dairy farmers' twoards dairy scientific activities in Jammu district (J& K state). M.Sc. Thesis, NDRI, Karnal.

Sengupta, T. (1967). A simple-Adoption scale used for famrers for high yielding varieties programme on rice. *Indian Journal of Extension Education*, vol. iii, No. 3, pp to 7-115.

Shah, Deepak (1996).'Working of milk producers' co-operatives in Maharastra, Agro-Ecomnomic Research Centre, Gokhale Institute of Poltics and Economics, Pune, pp. 169-170.

Shah, V.P. (1981). Role of milk cooperatives in articulating rural urban interactions:

Experience in Gujarat India, Ahmedabad, pp. 20.

Sharma, R.K. (1980). A study of socio-psychological and infrastructural constraints in the efficient execution of intensive cattle development project. Ph.D. Thesis, NDRI, Karnal.

Sharma, S.N. (1977). A study of the factors affectinga doption of hig yielding varieties of wheat of small farmers in Jabal pur Block (M.P.) Thesis Abstract 11 (3): 51-80.

Shatawdekar, M.V. (1979). "Adivasis around the Kosbad Hill" *Perinan*, vol. viii, No. 4, pp. 353-398.

Sheoran, V.K. (1987). A study of adotion level of dairy innovaitons in relation to milk yield among beneficiaries of IRDP in Karnal district, M.Sc. Thesis, NDRI, Karnal.

Sidhu, K.S. (1980). A study of dimensional variation in the knowledge of dairy famrers of ICDP and non-ICDP area of Punjab. M.Sc. Thesis, NDRI, Karnal (Haryana).

Singal, S.P. (1979). Artificial insemination under field conditions problems and solutions. *Livestock Advisor*, 4 (2): 17.

Singh, B. (1980). Planning strategy for tribal development in retrospect and pospects: A mid term appraisal from social adminstration development and change ed. Chaturbedi, T.N. and Chandra, S. K., Indian Institute of Public Administration, New Delhi.

Singh, G.N., Sengar, S.P.S., Singh, R.B. and Mishra, P.D. (1984). Impact of integrated Rural Develooment programme on agricultural development in Kanpur (A care study). *Indian J. Agric. Econ,* 39 (3): 477.

Singh, J.N. (1982). A study of the suitability of dairy farming innovations and factors associated with their adoption by cattle owners of Extensive Cattle Development Project, Gurgoan. (Haryana). Ph.D. Thesis, NDRI, Karnal.

Singh, K. and M. Das (1984). Impact of operational flood at village level. *Indian J. Agril. Econ.,* 39 (2) : 212-214.

Singh, Randhir (1989). A study of communication behaviour of dairy farmers regarding scientific dairy farming practices in ORP areas of National Dairy Research Institute, Karnal. M.Sc. Thesis, NDRI, Karnal.

Singh, S.B. and Patel, G.J. (1981). Economics of tobacco production in middle Gujarat. AICRP (Tobacco) *Guj. Agril. Univ.,* Anand Campus, Anand Res. Bull. 3.

Singh, S.B. and V.K. Dubey (1978). Adoption of scientific feeding practices of cattle owners of ICDP Karnal. *Indian J. Extn. Edn.* 15 (1) : 70-72.

Singh, Virender (1984). Impact of mini dairy scheme in district Karnal (Haryana). M.Sc. Thesis, NDRI, Karnal.

Somosundaram, D. (1976). A dignostic study of small farmers with respect of new agricultural technology and its effective communication for adoption. Unpub. Ph.D. Thesis, IARI, New Delhi.

Sripal, K.B. (1983). Tribal Development Programme - A Critical Analysis: Ph.D. Thesis, TNAU, Coimbatore, (TN).

Srivastava, R.M. (1982). Cattle culture and economy of Tribal Mundas of Bihar, Ph.D. Thesis, NDRI, Karnal.

Subramaniam, R. (1982). A study of technological and socio-economic impact of milk co-operatives in Erode district, Ph.D. Thesis, NDRI, Karnal (Haryana).

Tamboli, L.N. (1979). Training Needs of the tribal farmers in Relation to high yielding varieties of paddy: Unpub. M.Sc. (Ag.). Thesis, Gujarat Agril. Univ. Anand.

Thaha, A. L. (1975). Potensials and problems of Garhwal Hills Development. A Planning methodology, ed. V. R. K. Paramahansa (Hyderabad). National Institute of Community Development. pp. 146.

Tripathi, S.L. (1977). Institutional finance for IRDP-A case study of Sahar Block Etawah (U.P.) Journal of Rural Development. 2 (4): 470-473.

Tyagi, K. C. and Mishra, S.P. (1982). Dairy development problems: A perceptual reflection by the cattle owner. Paper presented in the XVIII Dairy Industry Conference, 1982. Indore, India.

Vaidya, A.R. (1977). A study on impact of Jayakwadi Porject in tems of changes in cropping pattern in Aurangabad district. Unpub. M.Sc. (Ag.) Thesis, Div. of Agril. Extn. Bichpuri, Agra.

Verma, M.R. (1966). Dairy husbandary of nomadic Gujars in six southeast Himachal forest ranges: A study in pastoral animal husbandry. M.Sc. Thesis submitted to HAU, Hissar, India.

Vithal, C.P. (1986). Factors affecting milk cooperative in Anantpur district Andhra Pradesh- A case study. Indian Coop. Review, 23 (4):

Vyas, N.W. and R.S. Man (1980). Indian Tribes in Transition, Rawat Publication, New Delhi.

Walia, A.P.S. (1984). Impact of Technical input services on the milk production enhancement in the milkshed area of Ludhiana milk Plant (Punjab). M.Sc. Thesis, NDRI, Karnal.

Yadav, S.S. (1986). A study of training needs of rural youth in Haryana. M.Sc. Thesis, NDRI, Karnal.

Vaidya, A.R. (1977). A study on impact of Jaykwadi Project in terms of changes in cropping pattern in Aurangabad district. Unpub. M.Sc. (Ag.) Thesis, Dv. of Agri. Extn. Bichpuri, Agra.

Verma, M.R. (1959). Dairy husbandry of nomadic Gujjars in six southeast Himachal forest ranges - a study in pastoral animal husbandry. M.Sc. Thesis submitted to HAU Hissar, India.

Vithal, C.P. (1986). Factors affecting milk cooperative in Anantpur district, Andhra Pradesh - A case study. Indian Coop. Review, 23 (4).

Vyas, N.N. and R.S. Man (1980). Indian Tribes in Transition. Rawat Publication, New Delhi.

Walia, A.P.S. (1984). Impact of technical input services on the milk production enhancement in the milkshed area of Ludhiana milk Plant (Punjab). M.Sc. Thesis, NDRI, Karnal.

Yadav, J.S. (1985). A study of training needs of rural youth in Haryana. M.Sc. Thesis, NDRI, Karnal.

Index

M

N

O

P

R

S

T

U

V

W